CEO *of* EVERYTHING

Also by Gail Vaz-Oxlade

Money Rules
Money Talks
Saving for School
Money-Smart Kids
It's Your Money
Never Too Late
Debt-Free Forever

Also by Victoria Ryce

By Me, About Me
MarketWise

CEO

of

EVERYTHING

Flying Solo and Soaring

GAIL VAZ-OXLADE
VICTORIA RYCE

Collins

Published by Collins, an imprint of HarperCollins Publishers Ltd

First Edition

HarperCollins Publishers Ltd
2 Bloor Street East, 20th Floor
Toronto, Ontario, Canada
M4W 1A8

www.harpercollins.ca

Library and Archives Canada Cataloguing in Publication information
is available upon request.

ISBN: 978-1-44345-064-5

Printed and bound in the United States
RRD 9 8 7 6 5 4 3 2 1

To my darling friends who got me through the tough spots and kept reminding me how much I was loved even when I felt lower than the belly of a snake. Even if you don't show up by name, know that I love you like fire.

And to all the suddenly singles who kept asking for a book of their own, this one's for you. —G

To the dear ones in my life. Every act of kindness, be it a phone call or a cup of tea, was recorded in my heart. Thank you for all your generosity.

And to all the brave and inspiring CEOs—if no one has told you lately, you're doing a great job! —V

CONTENTS

INTRODUCTION

We have been friends for years. Years and years and years. Between us we have experienced divorce and widowhood, and we have had to deal with the resulting "single" that attends when life doesn't work out just as we imagined. We both also have friends who have never remarried, never cohabited, never felt the need to join up. And when we get together and talk about being single, not a one of us moans or groans.

Yes, sometimes we miss having someone to share a morning cuppa. And sometimes we feel a little lonely. But when we put our singleness into perspective—when we see it in the context of all we gained or lost—singleness doesn't come up as short as many people might think. Well, not the way we do it!

If you find yourself single, what we say is CONGRATULATIONS! You got a promotion. You are now CEO of Everything. Feel ready for this new position? Don't worry if you want to shout, "NO!" Most people don't.

We got to be the CEOs of Everything having taken completely different paths. Victoria's husband, Michael, died over a decade ago. And Gail, well, Gail is the eternal optimist: she's been married (and now divorced) three times! So we know of what we speak.

Your path may be different from ours. But whether you decided to leave your partner, survived your partner's death, or discovered your partner had a different life plan, one that did not include you, now that you're here, you have to take control so you can make the most of the rest of your life.

In the corporate world, mentorship is one of the best ways those in the know pass on their knowledge. We want to mentor you to help smooth out some of the rough-and-tumble places on this road to a new life.

We know you can do it. You are smart enough to become a savvy CEO.

Now it's time to focus on the joy of singleness. While later you may decide to embrace the joy of partnering again, for now you're single and completely in charge of what comes next.

Being successfully single means not waiting for an event to trigger your joy in living. Being successfully single means not suspending your life while you wait for another to fulfill you. Being successfully single means accepting that you are the master of your todays and your tomorrows, regardless of your yesterdays.

CEOs don't expect miracles. CEOs know that change can be painful but that they can create the change they want to see in their lives. CEOs make things happen. They move towards their best life. And even as they do, they know that Perfection is the enemy of The Perfectly Good.

Sure there will be trial and error. That's normal since there are no perfect solutions, and each error provides you with information to let you make course adjustments. Have you ever met anyone who hasn't made mistakes? So don't be too hard on yourself. As long as you're moving forward, you're headed in the right direction.

We've had to counsel a lot of folks about picking up the reins of their lives and truly embracing the fact that they are in charge. In charge of everything. Every frickin' thing.

If you have become suddenly single, you may be in shock. Death can do that to you. So can a divorce that seems to have come out of nowhere (even though you may have been miserable for years). No one should expect you to be your old self. You may never be your old self again.

As CEO, when there is something that needs to be done financially, you are the decision-maker. When the car breaks down, you'll have to get it fixed. Most social life happens when you make it happen. Everything in the house is now your job: when the smoke alarm starts beeping, when the water stops flowing, when the microwave blows up, you must act. Grass will grow and you will cut it. Snow will fall and you will shovel it. The cat will puke on the carpet and you'll clean it up.

Everything now falls on your shoulders. Tasks you may have shared have all migrated to your to-do list. You'll do all the paperwork, make all the appointments, and pay all the bills. You are in charge of your whole world.

Sounds daunting, doesn't it? Perhaps. But being in charge brings freedom. Yes, it's a little frightening. But it's also incredibly liberating.

So if you are newly single, this is the book for you!

Whenever you find yourself in a new position, you look around for some orientation to regain your sense of balance. And that's what this book is: a guide to help you think through—and live through—the changes in your life. Even as you cry in your cups, even as you search for understanding of how you arrived at this place, there's a reality you must face: it's now all up to you.

Whether by design, default, or dreaded bad fortune, you may be wondering what you'll do first and then what you'll do next. We are happy to share our knowledge and experiences with you. We'll help you explore this new territory, highlighting key landmarks as you map out your new world.

We'll offer you guidance and support so you're not forced to tough it out on your own over every twist, turn, and bump. We'll eliminate some of the trial and error so you can move forward with confidence.

From the early days of being single to the changes you can expect in yourself and in others, we'll help you navigate. We'll show you how to take on the role of Chief Financial Officer, point out ways to replace missing employees, and help you rearrange your life so it can be all you want it to be. And we'll encourage you to reach out to others who are new to their own singleness and lend them a helping hand forward.

Single is not a death sentence. You may wish you could once again mate because you long for an ear to listen when you speak, or a hand to hold, or a smile to beam some sunshine into your day. But while you are single, don't hide from the responsibility, the freedom, or the challenges of being in control. This is your life. You must take charge of it. If you're lucky enough to find someone to share it with later, you'll bring new levels of competence and independence to your next relationship. In the meantime, step up. For however long you are on your own, you need to act like you're the boss. You are CEO of Everything.

Let's go.

1 · THE EARLY DAYS

Once upon a time you knew the general pacing and the track of your life. Some days you may even have functioned on auto-pilot. Things could be counted on.

Becoming suddenly single means you lose the rhythm of that life. You find yourself reactive, shaky about things you never used to be shaky about. You wander around in seemingly endless circles. No longer in flow, you wake up dreading what the day will bring.

VICTORIA'S STORY

When I walked like a zombie through the first few days on my own, I would at times wonder when the last time was that I'd changed my underwear, or brushed my teeth, or washed my face. It didn't seem relevant or important. Days were a blur. Here were habits that for nearly 50 years of my life I never thought twice about. Now I needed to actually think about them.

In the early days it may feel like it's nearly impossible to function. You find yourself gutted because you've misplaced your car keys or run out of milk. A notification of an overdue bill or a bounced payment throws you into a tailspin. You burst into tears because . . . well, because of just about anything anyone says to you.

Losing a relationship is hard. Your status changes. It's not just about checking a different box that describes you in a different way. You are like a child who has been through a growth spurt. You can't help falling down because your mind map and your body map are so different. You wake up day after day unprepared to deal with a rush of changes you never imagined.

You can adapt to your new status or you can fight it. (But fighting won't end well.) Moving forward happens by degrees. It means that today you'll willingly accept your new reality one degree more than yesterday. You'll acknowledge that your mate is not coming, or not coming back. You'll recognize it's time to take off your ring because it no longer symbolizes what it used to. You'll recognize that the traditional marriage and children aren't for you so it's time to begin living your life to the fullest.

No matter how much bargaining, promising, or pleading you do, you cannot turn back time, reverse what has happened, make it all the way it was. And no one should *settle* for a relationship just to keep a dream in play. You will mourn for what you feel has been taken. You will mourn for what you've given up. Even if *you* chose to leave a relationship, you will mourn.

Crying and confusion are part of the transition. You will get angry. You may try to rewrite history. You may wish you'd died instead of your mate. You may berate yourself for your foolish past choices. You may get physically sick. You may sleep for 12 hours or not sleep at all. You may hate everyone. You may think everyone hates you.

Expect the full spectrum of emotions. You don't have to apologize for them. Man, woman, or child, we cry when we are sad. (Some of us cry when we're happy, but you never hear anyone apologizing for those tears.) There's no need to apologize for your sad tears. As you move through this change in your life you may feel happy, mad, sad, angry, pissed off, elated, hysterical, or indifferent . . . or all of these in rapid succession.

Know, too, that you may feel unsupported in places you once felt secure. You will walk into a room by yourself and feel naked. You may feel alone in rooms full of people. And if you go someplace where everyone else is a couple, you may imagine a sign on your forehead flashing in neon: SINGLE. A gigantic shift has occurred in your life that cannot be wished away, intellectually reasoned away, or ignored away. It must be faced head-on.

You'll undergo two major types of shifts:
1. A physical shift: your partner is no longer there or you no longer live in the place you used to call home. (We'll talk more about these changes later in the book.)
2. A mental shift: you realize you are alone and must learn to deal with the emptiness. Or you want to rage at the world because you're a good person and this is so damn unfair! Or, with everything in turmoil, all you can do is worry, worry, worry.

MAKE A DATE WITH WORRY

If you find yourself single from divorce or death, you will be emotional: shocked, paralyzed, released, overwhelmed, scared, bewildered. You may be thinking, "How much more can I take?" You may struggle with your reality, which looks the same but feels so different.

Even as you boldly step forward, you may tremble with worry. You'll probably do it in the middle of the night. But since sleep is your ally in the early days, you can't afford to have it stolen by your ruminations. Watching the destruction of your world play over and over and over again in an endless loop at 2:30 in the morning won't help you deal with your stress.

One of the biggest downsides of chronic worrying is that worrisome thoughts seem to invade at will. You want to take back control from that invading army of thoughts by setting aside a specific time to worry. Yes, you're going to schedule your worrying time. During this worry appointment, you'll think about what's causing you to feel anxious or nervous.

Why invite worry? Simple. Worry is going to show up at the party whatever you do. Wouldn't you rather it be on your schedule?

It's not as easy as simply making a date to sit and worry. The first step in effective worrying is the hardest: You must learn to recognize when you're heading into worrying territory and catch yourself before you get too far into it. You will acknowledge that you have concerns, that something is bothering you. Make a note of what you're worrying about so you can give it your full attention later. Then set aside those thoughts, because you have a specific date and time for doing this worrying. It is during Worry Time that you'll re-engage with those thoughts.

GAIL'S STORY

It can be tough spotting when your worry thoughts happen and cutting them off at the pass. It takes practice. I know. I had to take control of my worry demons or I would have had a horrible life. As a master of the worst-case scenario, I could ruin something wonderful before I even had a chance to start it. I remember lying in bed beside soon-to-be Husband #2, who was 21 years my senior. While other brides-to-be were planning weddings and honeymoons, my overactive worrier had killed him off and left me to deal with life without the man I loved. How would I know it was time to get up in the morning if I didn't hear the toilet flush and the shower run? Cripes! I wasn't married yet and I was planning the poor dude's funeral. I had to take things in hand. I had to find a way to be more in control or my worry instinct would rob me of all the pleasures life could hold. I worked hard at it. And you will have to, as well, if you want to learn to put worry in its place.

When you catch anxiety crawling into your blood, breathe deeply and say, "I see you, Worry. I know that the picture is scary. Let's talk about it this afternoon at four." Don't forget how you felt. You'll need that to get into the worry later. Take note, set aside the feelings, and move on to something that can distract you from Worry.

Once Worry Time has arrived, don't try to do anything else. You want to give the worrying your full focus. Think about the worry or worries that invaded your thoughts.

Think about why the worry cropped up. Was it valid? Was it random? Was there a warning you need to think about?

There may have been a real purpose to the worry: perhaps you've overlooked something you need to focus on; maybe you haven't done enough practising to feel confident. If there is validity to the worry, make a plan for how you'll take care of what has to be done. If the worry seems random and without merit, think about what else is going on that may have triggered the worry to show up in disguise.

The point of Worry Time is to put worry in its place. But it is also to study the nuances of your worry so you learn to understand it. You need to worry. And the way to worry productively is to set aside a time to do it.

Typical things you may worry about include the following:

- Will I have enough money?
- Where will I live? Can I stay in my home or must I go elsewhere?
- How will we pay for the kids' education? Will the kids be able to go to the same school?
- Will I have to go back to work?
- Will my friends stay my friends?
- Will I be single my whole life or will I meet someone?
- How will we share custody of the kids?
- How can I co-parent knowing my mate has a new partner?
- Will I become a bag lady or a homeless guy?
- What will I tell my family?
- How will I cope?
- What will people think?

- Who gets the dog?
- How will I pay the lawyer?
- Can I make it on my own?
- Will I have to declare bankruptcy?
- What will happen to our business?
- Can I afford the car?
- Who will help me with my aging parents?
- Will I ever be able to retire?
- Where will I spend the holidays? Will I be alone?
- Does everyone know about my mate's infidelity?
- Does everyone know about my infidelity?
- Why did I make such stupid mistakes?

Sit down quietly with a pen and paper. Write down one of your worries. Then write the worst-case and the best-case outcomes. These thoughts travel through your mind, consciously or subconsciously, so get them down on paper so they don't haunt your dreams or keep you up at night.

Ask yourself what you can do about this worry. It is important to figure out what is within your control or influence and what you can do absolutely nothing about. No CEO spends time on issues that are completely out of their control. It wastes valuable energy.

Now jot down ideas of what you can do to deal with the worry. Let's say you're worried about whether you can afford to stay in your home. Your list might include these options:
- moving
- selling an asset to help pay down the mortgage

- taking in a roommate
- refinancing
- getting a second job
- asking for a loan from relatives or friends

Don't discard any idea. Instead, think about opening up possibilities. You want to give yourself the biggest range of choices, especially if you *feel* you do not have much choice.

Worrying is good. It's the opposite of avoidance. Avoiding tough decisions is a way of maintaining a delusion.

VICTORIA'S STORY

Did I want to give up my dream house on the water in the country? No way. Michael and I lived in paradise and finished the renovations to our century home just as his illness hit. But after keeping the books for nearly two years as a single person, I knew I wasn't going to make it financially. I worried about my future. Then I assessed all my options. Selling and moving to a smaller home were my best next steps.

Is changing your life easy? Hell no! But after all the worrying and taking time to let the mud settle, choices need to be made. You will probably find that you need to make changes, and some will be painful. You will lose some of the things you've grown accustomed to enjoying.

GAIL'S STORY

I loved living in the country. I loved the wide open spaces. I loved the 23 acres of mixed forest behind my house and the hundreds of different types of birds that nested there. I loved the critters in my paddock: the horses, the pony, the llama. I experienced a huge sense of loss when I moved from what I thought was going to be my last home. Even now, when I think back to that little piece of paradise, I get a bit wistful. It was a wonderful life.

If you allow yourself to worry non-stop you invite illness and disease into your body. People often say their home is their biggest asset. That simply isn't true. YOU are your biggest asset. You imagine and make the life you live, you can generate income, you can care for others. And you must care for yourself. You are the only YOU you've got.

Worrying is part of the process. Skip it at your peril. Your tricky subconscious is worrying whether you believe so or not. If you find yourself in "just surviving this day" mode, that's not a long-term strategy. You will wear out with this intensity. You need to release some of the tension, and proactively worrying—and then proactively putting a stop to worrying—will help you do just that.

Be proactive about worrying and you can take those problems into your conscious mind and make decisions about your future. (Remember, no one can change the past, so if that's what you're worrying about, you're wasting your time!) We invite you to worry and worry deeply. And then get on with living today and planning for tomorrow.

As CEO of Everything, you set the direction for Me, Inc. If you hope someone else will come along and make your life better, ask yourself this: Would you want to hook up with someone who was counting on you to make their life better? That's a whole lot of responsibility, isn't it? And if no one comes along, will you find yourself 10 years from now still in suspension, waiting, waiting? Hope is not a strategy: it is a short-term wish. It allows the pain to subside for just a moment. But it cannot be counted on to deliver results. Only you can deliver your happiness, your satisfaction, your calm. Only you.

PROTECTORS AND PREDATORS

Just as in nature there are protectors and predators, the same holds true in the human realm. Protectors will bring you food, do chores without your request, and sit with you while you rage, worry, and cry. Predators eye your surroundings, survey what they want, and use your moment of weakness to gain power or property. Protectors want to give and predators want to get.

No need to become paranoid; not all the people you know and trust are out to get you. But you are vulnerable. And your decision-making skills are perhaps at their weakest. If you have a predator in your life, they will use that moment when you are distracted to their advantage.

VICTORIA'S STORY
. . . .
When I decided to sell my country home, neighbours wanted me to sell them part of my land at a rock-bottom price. But that would have devalued

my property and I needed all the money I could get. My so-called friends threatened to sue me to try to stop the sale of my property from going through. As I was dealing with my sadness and all the worries about moving, they added a lawsuit to my pile. I thought I would break.

There will be decisions that have to be made. If you receive an inheritance or a payout from an insurance policy, for example, you'll want to do something with the money. But this isn't the time to interview new advisors or—heaven forbid—take investment advice from a friend. You just have to park the money until you can think clearly about what you want to do with it: find a high-interest savings account so the money earns some interest without being locked up.

Ditto the decision about what to do with your home (see chapter 8) and how to handle requests for financial help (see chapter 5). As long as inaction is not putting you at risk, this is not the time to take big steps, even if people try to pressure you, which they very well may.

In the early days you either think nothing matters or you gather everything close as you feel under attack. Normal. Your once generous nature turns grasping. Your frugality exits and the floodgates of giving open. You are not quite yourself, so guard against too much action. Let the dust settle before you take any big steps.

ACTION VERSUS INACTION

Think about whether you are a run-towards or a run-away-from kind of person. Do you prefer to be pushed or pulled? Do you want to take care of business head-on or do you take a Scarlett O'Hara "I'll think about it tomorrow" stance?

If you find you're a take-charge kind of CEO, know that you are going to have to take some lessons in patience. Since you will be swamped with emotion, it's important that you take it slow and sometimes let others help you. Be careful about the commitments you make. Tell everyone that all plans are subject to change. Your "yes" is a "soft yes" and could be a "hard no" by the time it comes to getting together. Be willing to change your mind even at the last minute if that's what works for you. You may have felt like an outing at the time, but today the winds are blowing in another direction and you need to stay home. You aren't being a flake; you are doing what works for you.

If you find you are more like Scarlett O'Hara, know that some decisions can't be put off forever. Some can't even be put off until tomorrow. So you must make your decisions based on what you know today, working with the best information you have at this moment. Do not let other people make these decisions for you no matter how tired or how tempted you are. This is your life. You will live with the consequences. The decisions must be yours.

As you transition from where you were to where you will be next, accept that the past—what's behind you—is gone. Trying to dwell there won't work. Even though you do not know where you will end up, keep your eyes focused forward. Forward is where you will find a beginning, something germinating, something only in its infancy but headed in the right direction towards your new life.

What is behind you may be destroyed or in disarray, but what is in front of you holds all the promise of a wonderful future. If you feel you are free-falling without a parachute, it's just a feeling. Grab hold of something (or someone) sturdy until you regain your balance. Then move forward.

PEOPLE SAY THE DAMNEDEST THINGS

Remember the television program *Kids Say the Darndest Things*? Well, adults say the darndest things too. If you were raised to be polite (Victoria was, Gail's mother tried), you may feel you must answer every question you are asked, especially by someone older or someone whom you perceive as an authority figure. Here's the news: You don't have to tell anybody anything. And you should not let anyone cast your life in a light of their own making.

GAIL'S STORY
. . . .

When my marriage to my second husband ended, a friend wrung her hands and sighed, "Oh, what a waste!"

"Pardon me?"

"All that time together, and you've only got a divorce to show for it." Seriously. That chick thought the nine years I'd spent with that man were "a waste." And she said it out loud!

None of the time spent loving someone is a waste. And after all that time, you bet I'd learned some important things about myself and about life. The fact that the marriage now was more of a misery than a celebration in no way detracted from the many years we had laughed together. And to frame a decade of my 30 years in this world as a waste . . . well, really! The audacity!

(BTW, she ended up dating my ex-husband, so it turned out to be a good thing for her!)

You will not believe what comes out of people's mouths. If you are fragile it may feel like an intrusion, or it may feel like wilful hurt. But that's in your head. The fact is people say the damnedest things. Don't take it personally.

If you've recently been widowed, don't be surprised by the question "Did you have insurance?" If you decide to keep the house after the divorce, you might hear, "How will you pay the mortgage?" And if you're coming to terms with your singleness, there's the inspiring "How will you survive on your own?"

You may be asked if there will be support payments, who gets the house, is there another person, who gets custody, was there a will, or how can you possibly cope. And you may wonder, "Are they asking because they care, or are they simply nosy busybodies?"

Unless questions like these are coming from someone from whom you are seeking advice and the information will help in the decision-making, don't answer these questions. Like the old song says, "It's nobody's business but your own."

If you were a politician being grilled by the media, "No comment" would be your response. Try that. Don't worry about sounding cagey or even odd; people who don't need to know may not even realize that they are being intrusive. You could say, "How interesting. Why do you ask?" to turn the tables and give yourself a few seconds to think. We expect intimate questions from close family and friends. Everyone else can be told to scram.

How to say this nicely? Try "I'm going to be fine. I've got good people who love me who are helping me make the tough decisions." Or "It's hard to answer complex questions when

I'm feeling so fragile, so I'm not going to." Or "It's kind of you to worry about me, but you don't have to. I'm going to be fine."

People speak without thinking about how their words are affecting you. They see you and they know they must say something, but what comes out of their mouths can feel more harmful than helpful. Here are some of the most inane things people have said, along with the responses we and our friends have chuckled about (none of us ever gave these answers— we didn't have the nerve at the time), so when you hear these words, you won't be rocked by them:

You'll be fine. Really? And you know this how? You're omniscient? You've got it figured out? Crap! I'm not fine and I'm not sure I'll ever be fine again.

Time is a healer. And I need some time away from you to heal this hurt because, you know what, no amount of time is going to bring back my mate!

You'll get over it. Of course I will. But I don't need you telling me this just when I feel like my whole life has come tumbling down around me.

He/she is in a better place. He's dead! She's gone! Not with me. Not in a better place. Just gone!

You'll meet someone else. Because I can't possibly have a life that doesn't include washing someone else's underwear?

You knew this was coming. Yes, I did. But do you think knowing makes it any easier when it actually happens? Who did you lose this week?

You can't change it, so why not accept it? So true. And I will. In my own time.

I need to give you the bitter truth. Why can't truth be tasty? How about some support now instead of kicking me when I'm down?

You need to pull yourself together for the children. You think I don't see my children's pain? Really? So I'm a crap parent too?

When a door closes, a window opens. Can I push you through that window?

GAIL'S STORY

When I left my third husband, more than one person who watched me cry for what I'd lost said, "You chose this." It was true. I had chosen to leave a bad relationship. But that did not negate the mourning for the relationship I had lost. I did not leave the man I married. The man I left was different from the man I'd married, and the relationship wasn't working for him, for me, or for the children. So I did the hard thing. Being told, in essence, that I'd brought this sadness on myself didn't make me feel better. It didn't kick my butt so I'd stop feeling sad. It didn't help me to accept the new life I was engineering for myself. It just hurt.

When people say things that are thoughtless, you may feel outraged, devastated, deflated, crushed, furious, or numb. Perhaps only later, when the words have sunk in, will you react to them. To the question "What were they thinking when they said that to me?" the answer is "They weren't thinking."

VICTORIA'S STORY

At a social gathering I once attended, one woman raised the topic of widow fantasies, where she imagined her life as a widowed woman. Everyone in the group was married except me, who really was widowed. While several of the women talked about how great widowhood would be, for them it really was just a funny conversation, a fantasy. But the myth of the Merry Widow is often far from the truth. Ditto the Gay Divorcee.

The expression people sometimes use when dropping their verbal bombs is "I'm just telling it like it is." But that's not true. They are telling it like they see it and that vision may be very blurry and based on a lot of faulty assumptions. It may only be their opinion, but that won't stop them from lecturing you. Short of punching them in the nose and walking away, sometimes you can't do anything about their prattle. But you are in control of how you respond to said prattle.

If you hold on to the hurt, you end up living with the pain long after the other people have forgotten what they said. Let it go. The nitwits had no idea they were being jerks. Move on.

PRACTISE SOME STANDARD RESPONSES

"I heard about your sad situation," someone says. How do you reply? Do you want to body-slam the person, run away screaming, pour out your troubles, or begin blubbering? Dealing with difficult questions is not a CEO skill you ever wanted to learn, but here it is. You need to hold yourself together as people blindside you, often in public spaces, where you feel most exposed.

Family gatherings are a favourite place to ambush single people with "Are you seeing anyone special?" In your fantasy world you might want to say, "No, I'm too busy getting it on with everyone I meet to make up for lost time." That would certainly put an end to the questioning. But it might also leave everyone looking at you as if you had two heads. If you want to maintain peace, go with a more traditional response. If you don't give a hoot, have at it.

Even if friends and relatives are genuinely concerned and want to offer support, kindness, or condolences, the gas station isn't the place to do it. If you find yourself being asked intimate or awkward questions at inopportune times or in awkward places, here are some stock phrases to get you through:

- Thank you for caring.
- I appreciate your thinking about me.
- I am doing the best I can.
- I'm still standing.
- This is very new and I don't have an answer for you.
- Right now I am finding my way.

While you're out and about doing errands, even standard questions can throw you for a loop. Take "How are you?" as an example. This sets you up to tell the truth or to obfuscate so you don't end up vomiting your emotions all over someone's shoes.

You could go with "fine," but everyone knows it isn't true. You cannot be fine. Under no measurable criteria are you fine if your world has just turned topsy-turvy. But this may not be the person you want to share your current emotional upheaval with.

And the supermarket aisle may not be the right place. If you open up the emotional tap, you may not be able to turn it off, and you still need to get milk and bread. So a stock answer it is.

VICTORIA'S STORY

As I was coming out of the hardware store, a neighbour stopped me in the parking lot. "I won't beat around the bush. I heard Michael has cancer," she stated. To say the wind was knocked out of me would be an understatement.

"Yes," I replied. As she looked at me expecting details, I felt unprepared to say more. "I need to get home," I said and got in my car. I don't think I did my other errands.

Some people will take "fine" as an answer, but others will see it as the starting point to try to get you to "open up." They'll pry for details. You can pull out a standard response like "Excuse me, but I can't talk right now," and then finish pumping your gas and flee the scene. But you'll look like Bambi in the headlights. Or you could say, "Y'know, I'm taking it one day at a time," turn the conversation back over to them with something like "So what's happening with you?" and then leave at a normal pace and keep your dignity.

Practise your standard replies. Then you won't need to think about what to say. Smart CEOs take extensive media training so they can prepare answers no matter what's thrown at them. Prepare your replies and just keep repeating them to get through the difficult moments.

SELF-CARE

Feeling a little fragile? Wondering if your despair is glowing like neon all over you? Hey, if you're sad, you're entitled. But only to a point. Do you know what's worse than being alone and miserable? Being alone, miserable, and sick!

Take care with your health. While this sounds obvious, many people living through stressful situations become ill because they don't pay enough attention to themselves. When your routine is disrupted, that takes a toll. You may be getting up earlier to catch a bus to work instead of riding with your mate in the car. You might be trying to do the tasks of two with your one and only self. Or you may be so distracted by your grief that even the most common daily rituals get forgotten.

Eat properly. Grabbing chips and a soft drink and plunking yourself down in front of the television may be easy, but it's not a good long-term strategy. Eating properly means spreading out your meals across the time you are awake. A cup of coffee is not breakfast. You know that fruit, vegetables, protein, fibre, and dairy make up most people's daily intake of food. If you don't want to make a salad, buy one pre-made. Don't starve your beautiful and very busy brain. Drink lots of water to keep your system in top running order.

Sleep as much as you need to. It may feel strange if you are sleeping alone for the first time in a long while. Create a night-time routine. Make the room dark, keep electronics out of the bedroom, and get into a pattern of preparing to rest. Try to go to bed at a similar time each day. Take naps if that helps.

Exercise every day. If your routine is to get up, get in your car, go to work, and then head home, reversing the morning's routine, then you're going to have to work at adding some activity. At a minimum, go out for a walk. If thoughts keep bombarding you, learn to walk them out.

GAIL'S STORY

I hate exercise. Victoria once asked me, "If someone had a magic wand and could grant you one wish, what would it be?" I said, "To not hate exercise." So far . . . no magic wand. But I also know that exercise is good for me. So I let my wee munchkin of a dog, Tabitha, bully me into going for a walk twice a day. To find your motivation, you can go read all the studies about all the diseases a little exercise can help prevent. Or you can just get a dog!

You don't have to go to a gym unless you want to. You don't have to take up yoga. A daily 40-minute walk is enough to significantly improve your health. And it doesn't have to be 40 minutes all at once. It can be two 20-minute walks if that works better for you. You get a chance to see what people are doing with their gardens, and you can watch the leaves flutter in the breeze. And if you are really lucky, you will see a harvest moon so beautiful it will take your breath away. Get out for a walk and your brain will thank you.

If you're feeling washed out or washed up, it might be time for a little pampering. Your emotions come out of your body in one way or another, and while you may think you are holding it together, you might actually be creating a powder keg ready to blow. Getting a massage is one of the best ways you can release the tension. When a massage therapist manipulates your muscles, it releases the pressure you've been carrying. And just the sensation of touch is healing.

VICTORIA'S STORY

Eliza goes for a biweekly massage because for one hour her only responsibility is to lie there. She doesn't have to make a decision or look after anyone or anything. It helps her mind, body, and soul to be cared for. She says she is worth it.

It's a funny thing, this idea of care. You may have been the one holding it all together throughout the sickness, the death, the separation—whatever has brought you to this new place. And then the worst does happen and, if you're very lucky, some kind people will step in to take care of you. But eventually, the people who are helping you through this period of crisis or change will go back to their own lives. And while you may have been great at looking after others, you could find yourself at a loss when it's time to take care of yourself. You may even feel you are being selfish.

GAIL'S STORY

As a single mom, Lynne had a roster of 16-year-old babysitters on speed-dial for those times she just had to get away. "It's Saturday afternoon. We just got back from swim class. I'm tired of all the ankle-biters. The volume is too loud. And even if I just want to go for a walk, I need someone to step in for me. I had to hire a lot of people so I didn't go crazy."

Finding things that pamper you in times of stress is important. It is an important part of your independence now that you're Executive Vice President of Human Resources, with the most important human resource being you. So, right now, grab a paper and pen and make a list of the things you love to do, the things that make you say, "Ahhh." They can be as simple as taking a nap or as orchestrated as soaking in a hot bath with lavender oil, surrounded by candles, a chocolate at the ready, a glass of wine at hand, and your favourite music lulling you.

Go ahead, we'll wait.

So what did you put on your list? Getting a mani-pedi? Hiking, kayaking, or batting a ball? Meditating? Heading to the library to pick up a mess of novels or a batch of DVDs? Going to the gym? Listening to your favourite band? Sitting at an outdoor café on a sunny afternoon?

For each of us, "self-care" looks a little different. This list is about making sure you take care of yourself. You have a lot of work ahead and you need to be in your best shape. Caring for yourself isn't spoiling; it's self-preservation. Be as generous as possible to the newly promoted you.

CEOs know that one of their jobs is to protect their assets. Preventive maintenance is making sure you care for the very valuable asset that is you. Don't skip your annual checkup, semi-annual dental visit, or biannual eye exam. So much of good health can be encouraged with healthy food and regular exercise. And bad health can be avoided by going to a medical expert for a tune-up. Make sure you've got a good checkup and maintenance program in place.

BED

Bed can be a particularly tricky place. You're sleeping on one side of it and a vast stretch of unused space on the other side tells you how alone you are. Dreams turn into night terrors. You wake up crying, sweating, panting. Your heart is racing. Your former mate may even appear in your dreams. While you may come to dread sleep, dreams—good and bad—are the processing grounds where thoughts and feelings can work themselves out. You could try sleeping in another room for a while, but eventually you'll move back to your bed. So it's time to make it "your bed."

GAIL'S STORY
. . . .

I've divorced three times. Every time I've started with a fresh bed. I don't know why this was so important to me, but I was unwilling to take the energy I was trying to leave behind along with me in the form of my matrimonial bed. So I took other furniture, but never the bed.

When I separated for the third time, I went hog-wild. I painted my new bedroom in a colour that was decidedly "feminine." I got a new bed and added a feather topper, something my last husband hated but I adored. I got new pillows, new sheets, a new duvet. I sprinkled lavender everywhere. This was my new space and it was going to be exactly as I wanted it to be. No more compromises!

Each night as I got into bed I would say, "I love my bed. I love my life." I did love my bed. And, eventually, I came to love my life again. It's a great life.

ONE DAY AT A TIME

Assuming the role of CEO of Everything can feel overwhelming. You have more things on your to-do list than you have hours to do them. Well, that's how you feel. But just as long-distance runners must pace themselves to ensure they have enough energy to go the distance, so, too, must you learn to take life slowly, doing only as much as you can, living one day at a time.

VICTORIA'S STORY

When I became Michael's primary caregiver, I began to feel frazzled and unfocused. I can't remember when I created a list called "Daily Focus," but it still sits on my fridge door as a reminder of what is important in my life. Here is my list:

Enjoy morning meditation.

Take vitamins.

Exercise, especially with dogs.

Eat fruits and vegetables.

Clean one room.

Throw away, recycle, or fix something.

Laugh, especially with Michael.

Be in contact with family and friends.

Read.

Try something new.

Do something for someone else.

Complete evening meditation and gratitude writing.

Enjoy morning meditation. I read this every morning (yes, the same one) and have for over 10 years. It grounds me.

Take vitamins. My health is important.

Exercise, especially with dogs. Exercise seems to be the item that drops off many people's lists when times become chaotic. Everyone needs fresh air and fitness, so I get outside every day.

Eat fruits and vegetables. Eat at least five servings a day, but you knew that.

Clean one room. Instead of making myself hysterical with the idea of cleaning the whole house, I pick just one room each day. It makes things manageable, and in about a week the entire house is clean.

Throw away, recycle, or fix something. I use this as an antidote to buying and as a reminder to myself to remain resourceful.

Laugh, especially with Michael. Laughter is another item that dropped out of my world when illness arrived. I know laughter is the best medicine, and now I look for funny moments daily.

Be in contact with family and friends. I am very grateful for my gang.

Read. Books have been my go-to source for many years. In times of trouble, I look to them to expand my knowledge.

Try something new. When I am stressed, I look for safe and familiar items. However, life is about growing, and I encourage myself to try new things. It can be something small, like a recipe, or large, like planning a trip; trying new things gives me confidence.

Do something for someone else. Here is where I move outwards from my own world. In difficult times I can shrink and retreat. By focusing on what others need and helping them, I keep connected.

*Complete evening meditation (*yes, the same one for over 10 years*) and gratitude writing.* When I write about what I am grateful for—be it a person in my life, like Gail, or the moon, or my good health—and I read a calming, familiar meditation, it makes for a lovely way to end my day.

A focus list grounds you and starts routines, something you desperately need right now. Consider the clean-one-room focus. You may think, if you have the vacuum out anyway, why not do the entire place? But just looking at the vacuum may seem overwhelming to the point where no room ever gets cleaned. Think in bite-sized pieces. You want the things on your list to be easily accomplished so you can feel good about yourself. That'll boost your confidence, which is very important in those early days when even getting out of bed may seem like a win.

It's time to start building your own daily focus list. As various demands push and pull you, this list is your touchstone of how you wish to live. Many things will vie for your attention now that you are CEO of Everything. Your focus list will help you see what to prioritize, what to say yes to, and what to turn down.

Don't think that you'll build this list in one sitting. Instead, start by writing down three things that you want to have as part of your daily routine. Just three things. Tomorrow, if you think of a fourth, add it. Next Tuesday, if a friend suggests something that strikes a chord with you, or if you read about something that resonates, add it to your list. Over time, you will build a focus list that reflects what's most important to you.

As CEO you don't need to justify your decisions. It's your life. You make it what you want it to be. Never mind what other people think you should be doing. Sometimes you must have the courage to go against popular opinion to create the life you want. As you bravely handle the various elements of your life, remind yourself that you are doing your best.

GAIL'S STORY

I don't have a list like Victoria's. She's way better at organization and follow-through than I am. But I do make a habit of saying thank you for something as often as I can. I'm a big believer in wanting what I have and appreciating even the smallest joys: a new bloom, ice glistening on the road as I walk Tabi, a hug from a dear friend. And on those days when I am seriously tested, I make a point of finding something PDQ to say thank you for.

When my last marriage dissolved—the love of my life was gone and I had to deal with it—I was so, so sad. It took many, many months to regain my sense of balance and find my happiness. And it took work. First I had to figure out what was making me so unhappy. Sure, it was easy to blame the split-up, but that wasn't actually it. My "not happy" was coming from a place far deeper. It was the sense of loss of my great love that was holding me down. And if I didn't accept the loss and find a way to remember what was good about my relationship and how much I had enjoyed it, I wouldn't find my happiness again.

I have a big laugh. But I realized that I hadn't laughed in almost two years. So I had to go find my laugh. Every day I'd search online for a comedian, a joke, a somethin' or 'nother to make me smile, giggle, guffaw! It took a while, but it worked. As I remembered how to laugh, I laughed more and more until I was full of laughter again.

BIG LOSSES

If your mate has died or gone away, you may feel like you've lost everything. Don't turn into a turtle. Turtles pull in their heads, tails, and limbs. They hide in their shells and do not budge. They are alone and distrustful of what's outside their immediate surroundings. Afraid or in pain, they have no capacity to deal with the world.

Don't pull in and hunker down; it will not help you to heal. Mates are the co-keepers of our memories. When they go away, we don't have that person to whom we can turn and say, "Remember when . . . ?" That's gone. It is heartbreaking. But it doesn't have to be like that forever.

As you jumble through your slow acceptance of your life as a single person, look for someone who has experienced a similar loss or has lived singly for a while. They can be your guide, having trod the path you've just started down. Let them share their hard-earned wisdom. They cannot fix anything for you, but they can help you see the world through the eyes of a person who went through this journey and came out the other side.

When you become suddenly single, it is like joining a club you didn't want to be a member of and having to fashion a new life. Once you accept that you are CEO of Everything, what comes next is both fear and excitement. Fear that you must do it alone and excitement that you alone get to remake your life in exactly the way you wish. You direct your destiny.

Be kind to yourself because you are taking in a lot of information in a short period of time. You may feel you are in a new reality. You are witnessing your own emergence into the role of CEO.

KEEP A NOTEBOOK

If you were a caregiver and your darling one died, you have lost your job making all the decisions you used to make. Now there is an entirely new set of decisions that need to be made. Becoming single—through death or divorce—means the rhythm of your life has been disrupted. With hundreds of decisions still to be made, you will forget things unless you write them down.

GAIL'S STORY

Benita lost her husband to a motorcycle accident when she was in her early 30s. When I heard about this I did two things: I cooked, because I wanted to make sure she ate. And I handed her a notebook and said, "Write everything down. You're going to forget, so write it down." Later Benita told me that the notebook saved her life. So many things would have slipped through the cracks.

Decision overload is common in the early days. You have only so much capacity to weigh choices, direct others, and figure things out. Most people have a limit on the number of decisions they can make in any single day. As your day progresses, you will probably become worn out, rundown, and incapable of even deciding what to eat for dinner. Get ready to say, "I can't decide right now."

Ideas will pop into your mind and out again. Your memory will fail you as your emotions use up so much of your energy. You may never before have forgotten a dentist appointment, but you may do so now if you don't write it down. You may forget to eat or forget that you've already eaten. "Let me check my notebook" should become your go-to line.

GETTING YOUR FOOTING

In the early days of accepting your life as CEO of Everything, it may be two steps forward, three steps back. That's how healing works. One day you'll rail against the unfairness of your circumstances and the next you'll say, "It's just fate." Vacillation is the name of the game.

If you cry, you don't have to make excuses for your tears. You are distraught; tears are normal. Don't feel you need to show the world how quickly you can bounce back. On occasion people will visit and begin to cry as they feel both your loss and their own. This will probably set you off crying again. Sharing those tears is part of the process of working through your grief.

You may be confused, stressed, uncertain. You may not yet be conscious of what you still have because you are focused on what has gone missing. These early days are the most daunting. You will be disoriented. But these days are practice sessions for dealing with the rest of the change that is coming your way.

You may feel dazed and your routines will be disturbed. You are leaving one world and entering another. There will be times when you feel extremely uncomfortable. Stay in that feeling without believing you have to fix everything right now. Handle only the basics of self-care and any immediate decisions that must be made. Everything else can wait.

Be kind to yourself as you navigate this new, unfamiliar territory. Know that just because you don't understand something today, it doesn't mean you'll still be in the dark tomorrow. You'll gain more clarity every week the more you practise being CEO. And one day you'll look back and marvel at just how far you've come (we promise).

While you'll want the choices you have to make to be obvious, most aren't. And some involve risk. The word "decide" means "to cut off." By choosing one path, you abandon another. So making a decision can be agonizing. The very idea of cutting off those other options may threaten to paralyze you. That's how you end up making no decisions at all, not even those you used to associate with routine self-care. Should you shower this morning or wait until this afternoon? Should you eat breakfast first or go for a walk? Will you return the calls you couldn't handle yesterday or put off speaking to people for another day?

Part of getting your footing back is realizing you lost it. You can stop flossing your teeth for a while, but three weeks is a new pattern setting up to take hold; you need to end it before it becomes entrenched. Ditto eating too much or too little, isolating yourself, or drinking yourself to sleep at night.

People sometimes turn to alcohol or drugs to dull their pain. If you say, "I just need something to take the edge off," that's fine . . . a couple of times. What's not normal is to go completely off the deep end. Trying to numb your pain with booze, drugs, sex, or food won't end well. Doctors call it "self-medicating." Eventually you must sober up, wake up, look in the mirror, and face your loss. Becoming suddenly single means you must come to terms with your new reality.

Don't criticize yourself when you see where you've stumbled. Figure out what you have to do to regain your footing and then do it. As you take on this new role of CEO of Everything, you will have good days and days that are not so good. You'll wake up feeling strong one day and want to crawl back under the covers the next. This is a process. You've begun. And as time passes and you deal with things one day at a time, you'll grow into the role. Have faith in yourself.

There are circumstances in which you can prepare for becoming single, although you might not think of it that way. Here are some ideas.

IF YOU HAVE TIME BEFORE A DEATH

Receiving a diagnosis of a terminal disease is devastating.

VICTORIA'S STORY

My husband, who used to run marathons, felt sluggish over the winter holidays. We'd moved back to Ontario from Quebec and tried to get a new doctor. I called every week until the magic moment when I heard "yes" and booked him the earliest appointment. After doing tests, the doctor phoned at 10 one night to say they had found a cancerous tumour in my husband's lung. Referral to a specialist resulted in treatments and surgery, but we were told this cancer was terminal. It was 13 months from the diagnosis to his death.

When a doctor tells you and your partner to get your affairs in order, you know that there is no time to waste. If you don't have a will, get to a lawyer immediately. If you have a will, make sure it is current and contains your up-to-date wishes.

End-of-life plans need to be securely in place. Even if this is the time when you feel least able to cope with making plans—you are sick or your mate is sick and you are panicking—you must. Working on little sleep and lots of adrenalin, you may feel exhausted by these decisions. Your brain will be consumed with bad thoughts that run through it like wildfire. It doesn't matter. You must act.

It's time to squarely face the potential of death and be realistic in preparing for it. Putting an estate plan in place means taking care of business so that those who are left behind don't have to unravel the horrible mess—legal and financial—left behind, even as they grieve.

You need a lawyer who specializes in estate planning, particularly if you don't have a vanilla-flavoured family. Don't use a will kit. Don't print forms from the internet. Don't use a generalist lawyer who does it all. Estate law is complex, and you need someone who understands it and keeps up with the legal changes so you know your family is well protected.

Some wills are simple. If it is just you and your mate, the estate plan can be completed quickly and easily. But if you have a complex family—multiple marriages and a passel of children in all their iterations—your estate plan will also be complex.

Your first step will likely be to fill out an estate-planning document, which includes a list of current assets like investments and pensions, as well as obligations, such as dependents and debts, and shows a list of all family members. All conversations begin with this document. Your lawyer will then make suggestions on how to make it easier for the surviving mate, children, or the estate.

The work involved in settling an estate is onerous. Putting the right legal documents in place can make it less so. (We'll talk more about this in chapter 5.)

Estate law is a provincial affair and the rules vary. But there are laws built into the system that are designed to protect family members, and your estate lawyer can help you navigate the rules.

One thing a good estate lawyer will do is remind the person making the will about their responsibilities to their current spouse, as well as to minors and adult children. Anything that can be made a joint asset will reduce paperwork and probate costs later. Decisions need to be put in writing, especially those that relate to financial issues and end-of-life care. Arguments between family factions at the bedside make for great television drama and terrible reality.

If you are in a blended family and you choose to distribute your estate in a way that may cause confusion, uncertainty, or even anger, make sure you have a conversation while you're still alive. Leaving this undiscussed until after you have shuffled off this mortal coil is the chicken's way out. It's your money. You get to do whatever you want with it (assuming you don't break any laws). But it is only fair to let beneficiaries know who will be getting what under the terms of the will. Unequal distribution to siblings will feel unfair unless they know why. Beneficiaries don't have to agree or even like what you're doing, but they do deserve an explanation.

People who consider not having a will as some kind of reverse talisman that will protect them from dying are dopes. For heaven's sake! This is not voodoo. You may not want to think about your demise, but dying without a will adds despair to an already devastated surviving partner or family. It could mean the loss of thousands of dollars. It could cause the court system to display your family's dissatisfaction, disorganization, and conflict for years. This strain is completely avoidable if you provide a clear list of your wishes. The little time it takes now will save months, even years, of untangling later.

Be completely clear about your wishes. Leaving things vague is an invitation to confusion and strife. Clarity is everything.

While you're at it, plan your funeral. The last thing you want your family to have to do when they hear of your ultimate demise is go shopping. What could be more difficult than trying to pick out the right coffin, urn, whatever, while also figuring out how to cope with your absence?

VICTORIA'S STORY

Wendall had lived with partners twice but never married. We talked about our end-of-life choices. "I've always been a planner and knew I needed to plan my funeral. I didn't want my relatives to have to deal with these decisions when I really wanted them to focus on how much they missed me," he joked. "I've got my brother and a nephew—see, I chose different ages— as co-executors. They know the name of my lawyer and where the documents are for my cremation. I want my ashes spread at the cottage so I can always enjoy the view." I wish more people were like Wendall. Unfortunately, only about half of us have a will and fewer have made their wishes known to family and friends. It's a shame we don't talk more about this. It would make it so much easier on those left behind if they knew what the plan was.

The average cost of a funeral runs to about $6,500. You can save a bit of money if you plan ahead and treat the purchase of your funeral arrangements exactly the same as any other major purchase. Figure out what you really want and then shop around for the best price.

SEPARATION: WHEN YOU ARE LEFT

Being left brings out the worst in most people. It feels like the betrayal will never go away. The loss can be sudden and shocking. You will get incredibly sad or unbelievably angry. You might turn into someone you never wanted to be, manipulating the children or painting the dissolution of your relationship as the fault of your ex. Even if you are in the right—the injured party—that doesn't change the outcome. You're on your own.

You may want your mate to suffer because you are in pain. Before you start plotting your revenge, remember that the time and energy you spend in this negative space is stopping you from moving forward to your new beginning. The emotion may seem necessary, but at some point you must take charge of it. You know all those stories you've heard about that crazy ex? How would you like it if people started plopping your name into those stories? Sober second thoughts are in order. It is not easy, but it is in your best interest if you want to heal.

Remember, all that crap that's running through your head is just that: crap. If you feel like people are judging you for the failure of your relationship, ask yourself, "So what?" No one can ever understand the nuances of another's relationship. And anyone who would judge you, well, you're better off without them littering your new life.

If you're feeling vindictive, if you're determined to get your pound of flesh, ask yourself this question: Do you want to pay thousands—or hundreds of thousands—of dollars to lawyers? Do you want to have the money to drive a nice car or pay for your lawyer to drive a nice car?

The average cost of a traditional contested divorce in Canada is almost $26,000 PER PERSON. And the most heated divorces cost far more. If you would rather spend your money blocking access, battling for funds you'll likely not get, or punishing your ex by dragging out the fight, know that this is money that you could be using to build your new life. And if you're using your children to beat your mate up, shame on you!

Your relationship is over. Hanging on by your nails is desperate and unbecoming. You need to reach some sort of agreement so you can get on with the next chapter of your life. Hold to the idea that you are the injured party who deserves their day in court and it will cost you big time.

Divorce doesn't have to be filled with fury and financial disaster. Leave the ranting and raving for your therapist, who'll charge significantly less than your lawyer. Better yet, rant and rave to your friends, cry on your sister's shoulder, get drunk with your best buddy. When it comes to splitting the assets, managing child access, and moving on, common sense must prevail. Mediation and arbitration are much better options than a contested divorce.

Why not spend time focusing on all the great opportunities you have now that you are single? If you are going to spend time thinking, why not think of what you'll be able to do to make your life just the way you want it? Of course you will feel the full range of emotions, including anger and pain. But if you let yourself stay angry and hurt, you're only making it harder for yourself. You have an opportunity to create exactly the life you want. And, who knows? Maybe in the future you'll want to send a thank-you letter to your former mate for giving you such a wonderful new life.

SEPARATION: WHEN YOU ARE LEAVING

Becoming single by choice brings its own set of challenges. It takes a helluva lot longer to get divorced than it does to get married. And it isn't anywhere near as much fun. All the planning that went into a big, honkin' wedding seemed worthwhile, while the planning to get you out of your miserable marriage seems like moving to purgatory. But plan you must if you want to make sure that your interests, and those of your children, are protected.

GAIL'S STORY

The first time I left a husband, I was in Australia. I climbed the stairs to an airplane, pulled off my wedding ring, and threw it across the tarmac. Then I spent years looking over my shoulder! The second time I left a husband, I made a list of everything I would take (including half the food in the freezer) and took only those things. It was a fast move because I was incredibly organized. The third time I left a husband, I had to pack for myself and two children. I worked all day, slept for three hours, and then got up to pack. (I didn't lose an ounce of weight, which I thought was damned unfair!) Thirty days later I was unpacking again. I got better and better at the process of leaving. But my last husband was the love of my life and the thing I could not pack and take with me was my heart.

Since emotions run high when relationships end, it's easy to forget important things. Get a notebook and write everything down. As CEO of Everything, you begin by collecting all the financial information you can.

Look at all the bills coming in and make a list of senders and their return addresses. Collect the contact information of stockbrokers, insurance companies, credit companies, banks, and revenue properties. Make copies of everything, including your property assessment, previous years' tax returns, Notices of Assessment, pension plan documentation, insurance information, wills, and trusts.

If you must delay your exit by a few weeks or months so that you are armed with the information you need, then suck it up and stick around. You have way more access to the information you'll have to provide to your lawyer while you are still in an intact family. Leaving prematurely—or booting your partner out too soon—could mean you lose access to vital information. Be smart. Be patient.

Leaving the relationship doesn't always mean leaving your home. (Never move out of the family home without first discussing it with your lawyer.) Will you stay in the family home or get another place? Will you be able to afford to maintain your family home on your own? Are you planning to move out of your old neighbourhood or stay put so the kids can go to the same school? Will you rent or buy? What will you be able to afford?

If you have a budget, you're going to have to do some rejigging. If you don't have a budget (what?!), it's time to make one. You may hate the idea of this, but if you don't have a plan for how you'll use your money, you'll find yourself getting to the end of the money before you get to the end of the month.

From the stuff in your home to how you want to parent your children, you have to be very clear about what you want. If you don't know what you want, what's really important to you, what you can live with, and what's not negotiable, the whole process will take longer, and cost more, than necessary. Know what you want and then be prepared to negotiate to get your "must-haves."

Since this separation is happening on your schedule, take care of some details before you heave-ho. Have a complete medical. Get your eyes checked and your teeth fixed. Get the kids done too. Tune up your car and fix everything necessary for it to be in good working condition. (While you're at it, check to see if it is titled jointly or in your name only.) Get yourself a new email address, cellphone, bank account, and credit card that only you know about. And order up a credit report so you can clean up anything that's messy. If you don't have a job and will need one, start looking now!

You're going to need a buddy network to get through the emotional upheaval that divorce will bring. One person you can trust is a gift. Two and you're less likely to wear out your welcome.

The next step will be to put a separation agreement in place. (More about this in chapter 5.) As you're taking care of the details of your separation, create a picture of your new life. What do you want to do? Where do you want to go? Who do you want to be with?

Don't forget to clean up the paperwork. That means changing the beneficiary designations on your insurance, pension, and anything else your ex-spouse's name appears on. If you had debt together, get your name removed from the documentation so that if the worst does happen and your partner dies or goes bankrupt, you're not left holding the bag. Make a new will and execute new powers of attorney. If you have a family safety deposit box, visit it, list the contents, and take pictures.

If you are moving, remember to redirect your mail so it ends up in the right hands.

GAIL'S STORY

When I left my second husband, he was really ticked at me. So when my tax return went to my old address, he tossed it into the garbage. It took me a year to discover I had a refund cheque that had gone uncashed.

Since separation can mean an immediate financial crunch, sock away some cash so you have money at the ready. As part of the separation process, you will be required to fill out financial statements for full financial disclosure. If you haven't been the guy handling the money, it's time to get familiar with what you own and what you owe so you can complete this paperwork accurately.

Make a list of all your assets. Identify whether an asset is held individually (and by whom) or jointly and the source of the asset, whether it was inherited or gifted to you, and when (prior to or during the marriage). If you aren't familiar with your mate's business interests, it is time to make like Sherlock Holmes. Create a complete list of all your family debts, including credit cards, notes, mortgages, lines of credit, and car loans. Identify when each debt was incurred, by whom, and for what reason, along with who has been making payments, and the monthly or annual amounts. If you're on the hook for your mate's debt because you jointly signed on his boat loan or her business loan, it's time to get your name off the documentation. Cancel joint credit cards to prevent large purchases by your spouse. Make copies of all loan documents, mortgage applications, and financial statements.

The more accurate a picture of your existing financial situation you have, the smoother your separation process and the better protected your interests. Once you've severed your financial connection you'll have to get busy creating your own individual financial identity (see chapter 5).

The Early Days will be the ones in which you feel least competent. Since you were used to being competent, this sense of ineptness alone is enough reason to feel upset. You've lost your footing. But please believe us: it is only temporary. You will regain your balance, your mojo, your clear sense of self. But first you will undergo some big changes as you transition into CEO of Everything.

IT'S OKAY TO BE SINGLE

There's often a perception that people are single because they have not yet met the person with whom they will mate. It's a perception that pervades how people respond to those who are single. It even affects how singles see themselves. When married people say they're happy, we know it's probably true. When single people say they're happy, we think they're cheering themselves up, putting on a brave face, making the best of things.

GAIL'S STORY

I can't believe the number of people who think that when I say I'm happy it means I'm doing "okay." Thing is, I've been in enough marriages to know that a lot of folks who are partnered are not anywhere near as happy as their Facebook pages would have you believe. From the inside, I've seen seemingly happy couples snipe and bite, hiss and spit, snarl and growl. I know partners who have bullied and partners who have been bullied. And I've watched more than a few married people weep with frustration, sadness, or anger. So I know "married-happy" isn't any happier than "single-happy." When I say I'm happy to remain single, I mean it with every fibre of my being. My girlfriends who have always been single sometimes wonder if I was happier being married than they are being single. I reassure them. While it's pretty normal to think the grass is greener elsewhere, learning to look at my own grass, and notice how great it is, has been an important lesson for me.

If you choose to remain single after widowhood or divorce, know that you're among a group that's growing and thriving. Time to re-evaluate how you're living your life so that you're doing what you want, and what you need, to be happy. That doesn't mean you're shutting the doors on ever having a partner. It does mean that you're no longer prepared to put your life on hold, no longer willing to drift, no longer worried that you can't have the things you want, if you want them badly enough.

GAIL'S STORY

Stacy had always wanted kids. After a couple of long relationships, at 37 she was on her own once more and realized that time was running out. "Even if I find a guy," she said, "by the time I develop this relationship I'll be well into my 40s, and having kids is not going to work." So Stacy decided to make her dream come true. "When I first mentioned adoption, my doctor said, 'They'll never let you adopt if you're single. Don't you know anyone who would be happy to impregnate you?' But Stacy had already decided that if she were to have a baby on her own, she'd become a mother to a child who really needed a home. "I'm still open to marriage," she said, "but my criteria have completely changed. I won't put up with crap anymore. Respect is a huge thing for me. I'm independent and I have my life the way I like it. So it's like me for who I am or hit the road. And they'd have to adore my child."

Those articles that report on how much happier married people are than singles are not a signal to re-evaluate your life. And when the first point in an article on being single is "Relax, it won't last a lifetime," just smile. Remember that while the upside of a relationship is social support, the downside of most relationships is that they come with at least some conflict and disappointment. You're choosing to swap cooking together for getting to eat exactly what you want. You're accepting that a mate's shoulder isn't the only place you can have a good cry. You know that you're going to be the one making all the decisions and bearing all the responsibility, financially and otherwise, and that's just fine with you. And while you may not have anyone to help you fix things that break or do the chores, you also don't have to suffer the frustration of being labelled a nag.

One of the toughest parts of being determinedly single is telling the people you love (or even perfect strangers) that you're fine with the status quo. Instead of feeling awkward at social events where there are mostly married people, find a body to take along with you.

GAIL'S STORY

When my nephew was getting married, I invited my girlfriend Boo to come along as my date. Boo was between relationships, but I know that even if she'd been dating someone she'd have dumped her for the weekend to come party with me. We screamed, "Road trip!" and headed to O-Town, where we had a fabulous time. Surrounded by all my children, I danced until after midnight, a major thing for a chick who usually hits the hay by 9 p.m.

Don't fall into the trap of thinking your life is humdrum and predictable because there's no one there to spark it up. Almost everyone knows someone who lives for spontaneity; let that be the person who sparks your adventures.

Revel in the time you have to yourself. Your married friends would give their eye teeth to be able to sit and read, cut up an apple and cheese and call it dinner, or stream four hours of the latest hit show on Netflix. Take care of yourself. With no one to spoil you, it's your job to indulge yourself. And make sure you build a strong personal economy. As the person solely in charge, it's up to you to make sure you're doing the detail so your life is not only happy and healthy but financially secure.

2 · CHANGES IN YOU

Do you know that old saying "The only thing that is constant is change"? That's your life right now. And with all the change *around* you, you also have to be prepared for the change *in* you.

It won't happen in a blinding flash. Nope. In all likelihood the first thing you'll do is freeze. Confronted with the shock of your changed life, or changed understanding of your life, you're going to have to pause and take a breath. Or two. Then you'll begin to thaw and start communicating about what you need. You'll move forward into your new life. It's a life that has been disassembled, like a Lego toy. Now, it'll be up to you to put the pieces back together in a new way. Be patient. And don't be surprised if the stress increases before it decreases.

The following changes may begin immediately or after the early days have ticked by. You may think you have had a chance to get used to your new life role or you may have rushed head-long into all kinds of feelings simultaneously. We'd like to tell you that it's a nice, even progression. But it can be a crap-storm of events and feelings, and you might not know which way is up for a long time.

FREEZING

If you wake up feeling insignificant, downtrodden, or broken, know that that emotion is in your mind. While it feels real, it isn't. It's a belief. If you allow those thoughts to keep running through your head, they will stop you from moving forward.

Limiting beliefs make you less than you could be. And they don't just affect how you see yourself; they limit how you perceive others. From "I've never been good with money" to "He didn't return my call, so he's ignoring me," the limiting beliefs that run through your mind are like stop signs. You have to push past them if you don't want to stay frozen. Whether you use visualization, positive affirmations ("I am creative"), or you fake it till you make it, you can trim the negative so that new positive beliefs have space to grow.

You may have regrets—things you wish you could do over. Yet your mistakes shape you. You are wiser having seen the consequences of your actions (or inactions). You cannot change what you did yesterday. You can only change what you end up doing today.

Knowing what you'd change is the answer to "Did you learn the lesson?" Spending time whining about what's wrong with your life or the mistakes you may have made doesn't get you closer to where you want to be next. But knowing what not to do again . . . that's priceless.

If you find yourself spiralling into regret, you're more normal than you may feel. But when you think of regrets, you must fill in the other side of the ledger: the joyful list. List everything you are joyful about so you're seeing both sides of any situation. That'll keep things in perspective.

The longer you live, the more do-overs you rack up because of all the lessons you learn. But the longer you live, the more you realize that the only person who can change what's wrong with your life is you. And experience's big lesson is that you can change what isn't working for you.

Depending on whether the change you experienced was gradual or meteoric, the acceptance of your new situation may take time to sink in. Your best friend is dead. Your relationship is over. The end result is the same: you are on your own. The acceptance of this reality takes time.

VICTORIA'S STORY

I recall freezing. The dogs would wake me up and I'd pull on some clothes to take them for a walk. I'd feed them and make tea. I'd spend hours on email and housebound activities. Walk dogs again, lunch, and listen to the radio. Dinner, then *Jeopardy* at 7:30 and one other television show. A final walk and then bed. I don't even know how long I did this for. My routine only changed when other people intervened. While my morning meditation says every day is a new beginning, it took me quite a while to believe it.

Don't think freezing means doing nothing. Watching television for hours and hours is a form of freezing, as is staying in bed, surfing the internet, or any other thing you do to avoid facing your life. Rehashing the breakup is a form of freezing. Reminiscing about the past is a form of freezing. It's a natural part of the process. So expect it. But also know that staying frozen means staying stuck.

THAWING

Thawing begins with being aware of what changes your moods. When you are frozen, you may feel numb or stuck in one emotion like anger, resentment, or sadness. When you begin to unfreeze, new feelings begin to emerge. Sometimes you'll feel like you're wading through an emotional quagmire. If you are enormously sad, you can't just pretend the feeling will go away. You need to work your way through the emotion.

Saying mantras is a great technique for dealing with unfreezing. When you catch yourself falling into an emotional pit, when you feel furious or frustrated, stop the thought and say something that makes you feel better. It might be a line from a poem. It might be a quote from a self-help book. It might be something a friend has said that puffs you up and gives you some juice. Swathe the negative emotion in the positive mantra.

GAIL'S STORY

I've used mantras for most of my adult life. I use them to remind myself to breathe. I use them to move out of anger. I use them to recentre myself when my emotions threaten to take control of me. One of my favourites is "I am the stone in the river," which brings to mind a picture that quells my rising bile.

I probably have a dozen mantras that I use regularly. Here is one I use with my daughter all the time: "Where you are today is not where you're going to be tomorrow."

If you're in a good place, you better say thank you and take the time to enjoy it since, in the circle of life, crap is around the corner. And if you're in a bad place, breathe and remember tomorrow is another day. This explanation oversimplifies what this mantra does for me. There is depth and texture, meaning, and strength in these words. They work for me.

Skip the guilt. If you have a long "should-have" list, it's time to rip it up, burn it, or roll it up into a ball and throw it to the cat. Maybe you should have saved more money. Perhaps you should have tried harder. Better planning, less drinking or eating, more listening might have produced a different outcome. But that's not where you are now.

There are times when we realize we have done something wrong, in which case remorse comes into play: we need to own up to our missteps, make up for whatever harm we caused, and move on. If you made a mistake, the point is to learn the lesson. Allowing guilt to manipulate your future behaviour isn't healthy.

Have you ever said to yourself, "I really should"? That's guilt. Why should you? Do you want to? If you do want to, then "should" doesn't come into it. If you don't want to, "should" is your guilt trying to talk you into it. Successful CEOs don't chronicle what they don't have or didn't do. They appreciate what they do possess, their unique skill set.

Unless you want to feel horrible about yourself, skip the guilt, brush regret aside, and get busy with your new life.

Start by making a list of what is going right in your life. Not in jail? Check. Enough food to eat? Check. A friend who will listen when you need an ear? Check. You've got things to be grateful for. Get busy being grateful.

Everything you use to distract yourself from your feelings— and ultimately the healing that can only happen by dealing with them—leaves you in the grip of your emotions. Feeling anxious is no reason to eat a tub of chocolate ice cream or go online and shop. Being so angry you want to smash things doesn't mean you throw away items to eliminate the memories, or trash-talk the person who left to anyone who will listen.

If you stay focused on what's not working in your life, if you sit and complain, or ask, "Why me?" you will sink further and further into misery. Misery begets misery. Ditto if you surround yourself with people who are themselves mired in emotional gunk. Find a happy person to be with and catch hold of their happiness.

Don't focus on the fact that your mate dumped your sorry butt; say thank you that your children are healthy and happy. Thawing is about reawakening to what you have instead of focusing on what you have not.

Maybe you love to run, play squash, or swim. Go do it. Perhaps listening to your children playing puts you in the zone. Grab a cup of tea, forget the yardwork, and just sit and watch the kids play. Maybe it's sex; hey, rip a piece and get to a good place. Whatever you have that makes you happy, do it.

Counting your blessings has a way of moving your sightline up from the gutter to the sky. When you choose to focus on how lucky you are instead of what your ex said to tick you off, you choose the sky. Let your ex rattle around in your head and you're choosing the gutter. You. Are. Choosing.

Think about this for a minute so you can get your head wrapped around it. Make a list so you can see it. What distractions do you favour? Is that distraction helping you or hurting you in the long haul? Sure, the shopping is great now, but will you want to kick yourself when the bill comes in? And maybe zoning out in front of the television stops you from having to think about how you'll deal with the problem at hand, but after all the television watching, the problem still has to be solved. What can you use as a positive distraction?

GAIL'S STORY

I'm as good at denial as the next person, and as long as I keep whatever I have to do in my head, I can bury it behind the myriad thoughts I have to think in a day. But when I write it down I make it concrete, and I declare my intention to deal with it. So I've gotten into the habit of keeping a daily to-do list, and everything goes on it. Even thinking goes on my list. "Decide what to do about . . ." is a pretty standard entry. Since I'm a "completionist," I hate having things that are unfinished; once I've written something on my list it gets done, no matter how horrible it is.

When you begin to change your behaviour, you will feel discomfort. Perhaps you like being frozen because, even though you're stuck, it feels less painful than actually having to do something differently. When you thaw, you know you are beginning to emerge, even if some painful work still lies ahead.

DISASSEMBLING

Now it's time to do some of the work it'll take to move from where you are to where you want to be next. Before you can rebuild your life, you must first disassemble it to see what's worth keeping and what you're going to get rid of.

There may be all kinds of things rattling around in your head. Time to get them down on paper. Get yourself a BIG piece of paper or a notebook and get ready to write. You're going to list all the things you're thinking about in no particular order. Just write down every thought in your head. You'll organize it a bit later.

How will I find sexual satisfaction?

Who will tell me I look good?

Will I ever be able to afford to retire?

Why am I here?

Who will rub my back?

What are my dreams?

WHAT IS MY PURPOSE?

What now?

Have I lost my allure?

Who will cut the grass, shovel the snow, fix the things that break in the house?

Where will I live?

What kind of work will I do?

Who am I?

What can I do for others?

Who will I talk to?

The next step is to get a fresh piece of paper and draw three columns. Label the columns as follows:

- Things Out of Reach
- Things I Influence
- Things I Control

Things Out of Reach. You're wasting your energy (energy you desperately need to deal with your own issues) if you spend time worrying about a global economic collapse. In your first column, write down all the things you are going to let other people worry about because they are smarter or more influential and may actually do something about the issue. Stick the weather in this column.

Things I Influence. You can encourage your kids to plan responsibly. You can set boundaries for how people interact with you. You can write to politicians with suggestions. So which things on your mind map are things you can influence? Write them down in this column.

GAIL'S STORY

I had a girlfriend who ended up divorcing in her early 30s. She had three kids in elementary school. I remember the day she turned to me and said, "I know I'm never going to have sex again." I looked at her, a little puzzled. She was beautiful. She was young. She had her whole life ahead of her. She declared, "My children come first. Now I just have to resign myself to the fact that at 32 my life is over." My heart broke for her, not because her life was over but because she was convinced it was.

Things I Control. Yippee! Finally a category with real potential for action. You control your spending. You control how well you hone your skills to keep up to date in your area of expertise. You control where you live, what you eat, and whom you hang out with. You control how you treat people, your attitude, and the steps you take to make the life you want. From your mind map, transcribe the things that are in your control into this column. This is where you'll place your focus.

Disassembly is part of re-engineering your life, so hang on to your lists. You're going to use them again later.

DISASSEMBLY VERSUS DESTRUCTION

Disassembling your life does not mean taking a sledgehammer to it. The reason you examine the pieces of your life—friends, stuff, thoughts—is to determine what to keep and what's no longer useful. This is more like surgery than demolition, so you need to be artful in what and how you cut away.

GAIL'S STORY

I have met so many people who, in the throes of loss, believe they have reached their best-before date. Once very attractive, they now see themselves as far less appealing. If they hope to partner again, they think they'll have to settle, since, well, y'know, they're not the freshest eggs in the fridge. And yet so many of the people who find themselves in single-hood are the warmest, most charming they have been in their whole lives. Let's face it, with maturity comes an authenticity most of us didn't have when we were younger.

You cannot do anything about your age. It's a fact. So your age isn't a problem, since a problem is something with a solution. Thinking your age is a problem could be the real issue. And taking a sledgehammer to your ego with negative thoughts about yourself—well, that's just dumb!

Don't let the tyranny of societal beauty standards bring you down. If you're tempted to say to yourself, "Look at that flab!" decide if you *want* to do something about it. If not, change your thoughts. If, when you look at yourself, you think your hair isn't straight enough, your complexion isn't clear enough, your teeth aren't white enough, you're thinking things that add no value to your life. These are the types of thoughts you'll want to take a scalpel to.

As CEO of Everything, you are the face of Me, Inc. That doesn't mean embracing the superficiality of looking like a supermodel. It means being true to you. If you want to make changes, go ahead. Get a makeover, join a gym, take a class, change your hair. But do NOT climb on to the Un-Merry-Go-Round of self-criticism. You will never be 21 again. Thank goodness. You didn't have the wisdom to deal with what life threw at you back then.

Just as you may be a harsh judge of your outward appeal, you won't always see your capabilities and competencies.

VICTORIA'S STORY

A friend watched me put fuel stabilizer in the lawn-mower gas before winter and asked, "How did you know to do that?" "I learned it," I replied, and he said, "You are so smart." I didn't feel particularly smart, but that is exactly what happens once you learn something. It becomes part of your skill set and you can't remember a time when you didn't know it. You moved around a corner of competence, only you didn't notice the move. When we are strong we don't necessarily feel strong. We feel in flow. Our lives just feel normal to us. Yet our skills grow daily by millimetres, and sometimes it takes another person to make us realize our progress.

COMPLEX SYSTEMS

Complex systems depend on all the pieces working well with one another in a specific order and at a specific time. Have you ever said, "I need to pick up the kids at the sitter but first stop at the store for milk, and then return the fan I borrowed from Mom and be home in time to cook dinner, before taking out the garbage, en route to a parent–teacher meeting"? This is a complex system. Without a partner you may feel dislocated, drop items, or run into bottlenecks.

You will need help. You will need backup people and backup plans. This is self-evident to others. But in your new role as CEO you may be trying to keep your complex system moving all by your lonesome. It won't work. With a missing employee, you will eventually grind to a halt. Literally. You may find yourself standing in the middle of a room unable to think what to do next. The can-do person you used to be didn't function in isolation then and won't be able to now. The kettle is boiling, the dryer is buzzing, the phone is ringing, the kids want lunch, the dog is barking, and the babysitter called earlier and cancelled. Now what?

Equipment specifications have a term for this: "maximum load." You've just exceeded your capacity. You can run screaming from the room. You can lie down and pull the covers up over your head. Or you can ask for help.

GAIL'S STORY

When I was leaving my last relationship, I was working full-time and packing for myself and two children and the household we would be setting up elsewhere. The timing of my move had been accelerated by circumstances beyond my control and I found myself with a moving day that also included giving a presentation that night two hours from my new home. So I called Brownie. Brownie and I have been friends for a thousand years. We don't talk more than three or four times a year, but we love each other. Brownie got in her car, drove to my house, and helped me throw the last of the stuff into boxes. The movers arrived and we guided them through what to take and what to leave. (I only took what I would use, leaving plenty behind.) Then we drove the 30 minutes to my new home. We unloaded. I showered, got dressed, and Brownie drove me into the city to make my presentation. When I was done, she drove me home again to sleep on the floor because absolutely nothing had been unpacked. God bless that woman.

One of the things CEOs are really good at is building and leading teams. As the person in charge of your life, it's your job to make sure you have a team that can get things done and that every member of your team feels appreciated.

Make a list of all the people in your life. All of them. They may not all be willing or able to help all the time, but some of them will be willing to step in from time to time to see you through a rough spot. You should have their names, addresses, and telephone numbers handy. If one is far away but is willing to listen to your late-night tirades about how angry or sad you are, that's useful to know. If another has a mate who is handy, add him or her to your team roster. If one can refer you to a good psychologist, a great plumber, or a willing dog-sitter, that, too, is good to know.

Ever tried to remove a sliver from your own finger on your dominant hand? It is nearly impossible. Even if you are used to toughing it out alone, asking for help may be one of the hard lessons you'll have to learn. It could take five hours to wash your windows by yourself, moving the ladder as you go. Or it could take an hour and a half with someone helping. (And then you can return the favour.) The same amount of work gets accomplished, but the experience is a whole lot nicer.

GAIL'S STORY

When I moved into My Little House I quickly realized there were things I had never had to deal with before. A tree fell down in my backyard during my first winter and had to be chopped down and dug out. Hell, I was NOT up for that. But my girlfriend had a husband who was, and I traded a dinner of crab cakes for his effort. Ditto when I had to have new light fixtures installed. (I am not good on a ladder.) But another girlfriend had a husband who knew his way around electricals. I came to refer to these loaned husbands as my "sub-hubs," my substitute husbands. Whenever I have something that's outside my skill set, I post a message on Facebook: "Sub-hub needed to . . . (description of the job). Will cook in exchange."

Most people like to be helpful. And, having asked for assistance, you've opened up the gates for reciprocation. Maybe they will ask you for help and you will get to feel good about helping out too.

While you will be tempted, in the initial stages of coming to grips with being single, to be self-focused, that's not a healthy place to stay. You've got to get out of your head and stop the constant replaying of your past in your mind. When you ask for help or help others you will move out of that pattern by creating a new interaction. It'll jolt you from your miasma, acting as a "commercial break" from the program that is playing on repeat in your brain.

VICTORIA'S STORY

There are small bridges running across a creek on my property. Over time the wood rotted and so one bridge needed new boards. I had some cedar that a neighbour offered to cut up if I measured it. When I arrived at his shop to pick up the cut boards, another friend was there and I joked, "If you don't have anything to do, you could always help me build a bridge." He came home with me, and in about an hour the bridge was rebuilt. It would have taken me so much longer on my own. And I learned a lot about how to assemble, space, and screw in boards. He left with a bottle of wine and some baking from my freezer. That's what happens when you're willing to ask for help.

You may be strong, but nobody can do it all. You are more connected than you imagine, and people like to help. It makes them feel worthwhile. So help them by letting them help you.

DISASSEMBLING LAMENTATIONS

Take time to lament what you have lost. It is part of the disassembling process. If you don't, it will become another item swept under the psychic rug, piling up until you trip over it at the most inopportune moment. Perhaps at a family gathering, suddenly you will burst into hysterical sobs and wail, "I feel so alone and lost!"

Better to handle this on your own terms: in the privacy of your own home, with a therapist, or with your best friend. Your life has been disrupted. You will be discombobulated. Breaking down is part of the process. Then you can rebuild, and rebuilding is what the rest of your life will be about. The feelings of disruption won't last forever.

The first time you fill in a form where you must write your new status may be painful. The 10th time you do it will be reflexive. Changing your Facebook status may trigger a flurry of activity as people seek to understand what has happened. So make sure you're ready for the inquiries or keep the information to yourself until you are.

In your heightened emotional state you will feel like everything is about you. It isn't. And you'll have to keep reminding yourself of that. As you look at the magazines at the checkout counter in the supermarket, it will seem like those headlines are speaking directly to you: "Eight Ways to Pick Up the Pieces." And more than one television episode, heart-wrenching commercial, or book will make you burst into tears. Hey, it's par for the course. Eventually you'll be fully disassembled and, having examined all the elements, you'll be ready to begin reassembling.

REASSEMBLING

And now the rebuilding begins. Many a CEO has been hired into a company to rebuild it. And as CEO of Everything, you have the option of reassembling the pieces of your life to make it just as you'd like it to be.

Remember the list you made earlier? Time to put it to use.

Take the questions, goals, and thoughts you mind-mapped and cluster them. Some big chunks might include things like work, health, relationships, obligations, and future security. What are the overall themes you see reflected in the pieces of your life as you would like it to be?

With all the Lego of your life spread before you, you get to build what you want. Time to decide what you want to keep and what it's time to chuck. Don't be surprised if the life you had and the life you want are very different. That's a change in you.

Perhaps you put "move to a new home" on your map. Start to list all the actions you need to take to prepare for the move. Will you buy or rent? What furniture will go with you to your new life? What clutter needs to be removed? What are you taking on your new adventure? When do you plan to move?

Perhaps you've decided you need to return to work. Will you require new skills? Do you have an up-to-date resumé? Who can you ask for references?

As you reassemble your life, you will experience successes and failures. Nobody gets it right 100% of the time. You will make mistakes. The nice thing is you can simply pull that piece out of the mix and decide where else it should go or toss it completely.

VICTORIA'S STORY

I watch people agonize over decisions they have to make as if there is a perfect choice and they just have to figure out which one it is. Almost always when people make decisions they have to do so with incomplete information. Hey, you know what I've learned from all my not-so-great decisions? If something didn't turn out like I expected, at least now I was working with more information and could make a different decision.

If you only play it safe, you will make your life smaller. Taking baby steps is fine. But don't stop dreaming. CEOs create the best conditions for their future by setting directions, knowing their values, and moving towards their goals.

Think about what you've always wanted to do and have never done. What's at the core of how you want to experience life? Will you travel down the Amazon River or visit Iceland? You get to determine if you'll live a big life or a small one. If you just allow yourself to float along with the current, bobbing and dipping, then one day you will wake up and wonder where the last year, last five years, last decade went. Become deliberate about what you want out of life. Do you want to get a degree or become a chef? You may not feel ready today to go the whole way, but you can plant and water the seed and watch the dream grow. If you want to visit Latin America, take Spanish classes. Do something to get ready for your next adventure.

VICTORIA'S STORY

I glued a picture of the Grand Canyon on a jar in my bathroom cabinet. I put my loonies into the jar because visiting the Grand Canyon is on my bucket list. With each dollar I add, I get closer to my dream. I see the picture and I reaffirm my determination to get there.

Take the time to notice when you are extraordinarily happy or content. What are you doing that makes you feel this way? Can you put more of it in your life? If you are not putting joy and pleasure in your life, who will? Remember, a key role for every CEO is to allocate resources, and one of those resources is time.

If your first instinct is "I just don't have the time," know that the minutiae of life will have won. Start thinking in terms of what's worthwhile and what isn't. You only have so much energy. You only have so much time. Are you using these resources to your best advantage?

Would you rather cook every day or batch-cook so you have time to read?

Would you rather spend time dusting or get rid of knick-knacks so you can spend more time in the garden?

Would you rather do everyone's laundry or teach your children to do their own so you have time to meet up with a friend for coffee?

VICTORIA'S STORY

I was at an authors' festival where I heard a writer say she had found time to write because she stopped cooking when her youngest child went off to college. "Kaput, no more," she declared. "Anyone wants food, it's in the freezer, or at the other end of the phone, or in a pot at the end of their own hands."

As you reassemble your life, you get to try things without feeling like they are lifelong commitments. If that new step class doesn't appeal to you, say thanks and stop going. If online dating turns into a joke, laugh and leave it at that. But don't avoid trying something new because you prejudge that it won't work for you.

Instead of welcoming a tyrant inside your head who always tells you why stuff won't work, install a guardian angel who loves you and thinks you are brilliant and wants the best for you.

VICTORIA'S STORY

I had a wonderful friend, Jacqueline, who introduced me to the joy in small things. She sent me recipes with little notes that said, "Top with toasted almonds to make them as pretty as possible because Christmas is special." She had a talent for appreciating the small things, like seeing a chickadee. When the critical tyrant voice enters my head, I ask myself, "What would Jacqueline tell me?"

Put things in perspective. Since some of your decisions will be of a more temporary nature, while others will have a long-term impact, when you are deciding something, ask yourself if it is a decision for today, this week, this year, forever, or until something better comes along. That'll help you see how important the decision is and how much time you should spend making it.

GRATITUDE

The word "gratitude" derives from the Latin word *gratus*, which means grace, graciousness, or gratefulness. People who are grateful tend to focus on what they have as opposed to what's "missing." Positive psychology research shows that gratitude correlates to greater happiness. When you bask in good emotions, not only do you improve your health, you improve your relationships. But spending time being grateful doesn't just make you happier; it can make you stronger too. Gratitude positively correlates with our ability to deal with adversity.

With payoffs like increased happiness and health, better relationships, and an increased ability to deal with challenges, you'd think most of us would spend some time each week counting our blessings. Letting people know how much they mean to you takes only seconds. Saying thank you with a smile and warm eyes can make the people around you glow. When you truly appreciate what you have, you will stop reaching for other things in the hope that they will make you happier, because you will, at last, have found your happiness where you are.

Keeping a gratitude journal may help you focus on what you are grateful for and can completely change your mood.

VICTORIA'S STORY

I have gratitude journals going back years. In a tiny calendar—you know the kind, with little squares for each day—I write three or four things I am grateful for each night before going to sleep. Even on the day my husband died, I wrote I was grateful for the nurses, grateful my stepdaughter was there, and grateful for the snow that fell.

At the end of the year, you'll see how much you have to be grateful for. It helps you notice what can sometimes fly beneath the radar. If you haven't kept a gratitude journal before, starting is easy. A small pocket diary or an ordinary notebook is all you need. Put it beside your bed, and before you go to sleep write one, three, or five things you are grateful for.

Maybe you are grateful you washed your face, grateful you ate lunch, grateful for your pet. Doing this right before bed is calming. And on days when you feel terrible and despise everything, perhaps you are grateful you didn't murder anyone. Hey, a sense of humour is a good thing. Be grateful for it.

GAIL'S STORY

I have a friend on Facebook who posts about the things for which she is grateful on Tuesdays, under the title "Gratituesday." Each Tuesday I watch as she counts her blessings. And as I do, I ask myself why more people don't share what they are grateful for in their lives.

MOVING FORWARD

Dates that once marked anniversaries, birthdays, and special events are now emotional minefields. If your partner died, the day of their death, along with their birthday and your anniversary, will be bittersweet. Bitter at first; sweeter over time. If you were married, the things you did as a couple—the planning for retirement, the sharing of special family occasions—will also be bittersweet.

It's time to let go of old markers and establish new ones. Things you celebrated before can be replaced by new things. There will be pain, particularly in the beginning, around the old "special" days. But over time you'll create new special days to focus on.

VICTORIA'S STORY

I received wise advice from my aunt Alexandra. We were shopping and she asked, "Would Michael have bought you something for your upcoming birthday?" Of course he would have. "Well, then we need to find something he would have bought you."

On your birthday or on any other occasion when you would generally receive gifts, go buy yourself something. Having nothing to open on a special date is a downer. As CEO of Everything, celebrating your special days is your job too. Rather than contemplating what you've lost on a special day, find a way to make the day bright for yourself.

GAIL'S STORY

I was the celebrator of events in my family. Birthdays, Christmas, anniversaries, I did 'em up big. Somewhere towards the end of my last marriage I realized that while I was taking care of everyone else, no one was taking care of me. The kids were relatively young (and did the lovely things children do, like make those cute crafts), but if there was going to be joy in my life, if there was going to be a celebration, it would be up to me to make my day special. I separated before my 50th birthday. Just about seven months into a new life, it was hard to celebrate that milestone—I felt like I'd lost so much—but I put on a brave face and invited a few of my girlfriends to join me for lunch, my treat. Since then I've learned that I can celebrate without the fuss I used to make. But I seldom do it on The Day. Instead, I celebrate around the day so that I'm not trying to outshine old memories. I do Christmas with my children before or after the actual Christmas week so we're not competing with other family obligations. And for my birthday, I make a list and go shopping for the things I'd like to get as gifts and give them to myself. (I'm very good to me.) I've learned that I'm as worthy of receiving a present from myself as all those other people who were receiving gifts from me back when I was the celebrator.

Don't wait for someone to invite you over for a celebration. Tell people you'll be on your own for the occasion and watch the invitations arrive! Pride goeth before a lonely night at home. Put your pride away and tell people you're available for a date.

Alternatively, have the occasion at your place and invite others over. It doesn't have to be on The Day—there's a lot of competition for The Day—but it can be just as lovely an occasion.

Accept invitations extended to you, even if it means cancelling later because you're really not up to socializing, or go but stay only for a short time. Your instincts may be that you're awful company or that you don't want to face the questions and the pity, but that's crap your own brain is making up. Go with the expectation of enjoying yourself. And if you feel partway through the evening that the visit is just not for you, then make your excuses and feel free to vamoose. Stay for as long as you feel good or comfortable.

VICTORIA'S STORY

Cara is a widow in her 60s. When she was asked out on a date, she hesitated. She said, "I'm not really sure because I am liking being alone. I have a great book I want to read right now." She did end up going out and had fun. They decided it was nice to have someone to go out to dinner with from time to time. He's gone to her house for a family gathering and she's gone to his place for Thanksgiving with his family. Cara's effort gave her a new friend to share special occasions.

Just as special occasions will bring bittersweet feelings, so too will things you do day-to-day that have emotional reminders attached. There may be music you can no longer listen to, programs or movies you can no longer watch, and other reminders too painful to endure. Time to make a new playlist, try new shows, start new activities. If you simply drop things from your life, you will find the emptiness just as painful.

Reassembly takes time and may feel strange when you begin. In part it is because you've forgotten the nervous feelings you had way back when you began what eventually became old, familiar traditions. In part it may be because you feel like you're creating a substitute for "the real thing." Acknowledge your feelings and try the new idea anyway.

LONELY VERSUS ALONE

Aloneness is not the same as loneliness, although the two words are often used as synonyms. They're not.

GAIL'S STORY

Some of my loneliest moments happened when I was in a room full of people. When I separated the last time, I fully expected to be swamped by loneliness. I wasn't. When first my daughter and then my son went off to school, I expected to feel lonely. I don't. What I feel is free. It is a remarkable thing to discover that you enjoy your own company.

I have now been living by myself (with Tabitha, my fur-baby) for enough time to know that I really, really like it. If I get lonely, I pick up the phone and call Victoria and we chat about books. Or I call up my girlfriend Casey and we make plans to go to the garden centre or see an arts and crafts show. Or I get on Facebook and strike up a conversation with a friend living far away. Distance means nothing to me anymore. And my time, well, I get to spend it just as I please. If I don't feel like cooking, I don't. If I want to indulge in a mid-afternoon respite, I cuddle up with Tabi and read or snooze. I have crafted a life that I love, and I enjoy the quiet time as much as the time I spend socializing.

You have the opportunity to make your life just the way you want it to be. Yes, you may have commitments that you'll always have to schedule—children, work, aging parents. But think about time like a large piece of fabric. You can snip away pieces to use for yourself, even as the larger piece is dedicated to your responsibilities.

Grab a piece of paper and a pen. Draw three columns.

In the first column, write down what you will continue doing in your new life. What has to be done? Taxes, laundry, and brushing your teeth will land on this list. What gives you pleasure? It may be reading to your kids, volunteering, or getting a massage.

In the second column, list what you will quit doing so you can make the first column work. Perhaps you'll forgo buying clothes that need dry cleaning so you can eliminate the toing and froing to the cleaners. Or you'll avoid malls and take your walks in the woods. Not everyone will be thrilled with your shift in focus. So be it.

VICTORIA'S STORY

Ever feel like you've become part of the staff in someone else's life? You can stop feeling like this. I had to learn how to say no gracefully but adamantly. Here is a script I use:

THEM: Hi, I am just calling about the fundraiser. We've got you down for cleanup, right?

ME: No, thank you. Not this time.

THEM: What? What do you mean?

ME: Let's give someone else a turn at helping.

THEM: But you always do it.

ME: In the past I did, but I'm not going to this time.

THEM: What's wrong?

ME: Nothing.

THEM: Something must be wrong.

ME: Actually, I'm good. But I need to go, so good luck with your fundraiser.

Remember how kids used to say, "You're not the boss of me"? Nobody is the boss of you. You can give yourself another assignment or take time off. It's your life and you decide what you're doing with it. Even if you have done something for a donkey's age, you can stop. You get to manage your personal time and your choices. Perhaps something has just become too much. You need to say, "Thanks, it was great, but good-bye." You are CEO of Everything and you get to make the decisions. It is one of the perks of the job.

In the third column, itemize the things you would like to add to your life. Perhaps you want to take a computer class, start riding a bicycle, or learn to paint. These are the things you anticipate enjoying, things you will use to fill those spaces that might otherwise be filled by loneliness.

GAIL'S STORY
. . . .
After an early divorce, Gemma has been single for most of her life. But she learned how to manage. She learned to fill the space so there wasn't

as much room for the loneliness. She took salsa lessons. She took acting classes. She tried lots of new things so she wouldn't stay at home being lonely. She made more friends, people she could meet for lunch or take another class with.

Sometimes it takes a specific activity to bring closure to your old life so you can commit fully to the new one you're creating. There may be some unfinished business with your partner, things you need to tie a bow on. Perhaps you need to do something symbolic?

VICTORIA'S STORY

Michael and I had always planned to go to Newfoundland. To honour his 60th birthday, I went there on my own. And you know what? I really enjoyed the trip. At the bed and breakfast I chatted with new people. When a couple from Boston asked me about driving to Cape Spear, I brazenly asked if they would mind if I went with them. It turned out to be fabulous. I swapped my knowledge of Canada for the car ride. We hiked Blackhead, visited Ferryland, and I treated them to lunch. Later we exchanged Christmas cards.

Being alone can lead to some of the sweetest times in your life. While you may have enjoyed being with someone, don't be surprised when you learn how much you enjoy being with yourself.

VICTORIA'S STORY

Marilyn was happily married for a long time before her husband's death. Recently she's been going out with a man who wants to get serious. "He wants to get married, but I don't. I just want the sex and then he can go back to his own place. I don't mind cooking some dinner first, but I would rather not do his laundry and clean up. He keeps asking me to marry him, but I like being on my own." For some people, marriage is the goal and for others, well, a little company once in a while is enough.

DISAPPOINTMENTS

Prepare to be disappointed by some of the people you thought of as friends. You may become a stranger to some people who knew you because you are changing. Others change, too, particularly in how they react to your new singleness. Try not to take the shifts in friendship personally. If you let it get under your skin, you may become bitter.

VICTORIA'S STORY

When Rosie's husband died, her sorrow turned to bitterness. If a person did something she didn't like, she would dismiss them with "Don't let the door hit you on the ass on your way out." Then she would tell her other friends about the conversation, trashing the former friend. Poor Rosie's broken heart had become completely intolerant and she couldn't see the good in anything. Instead, she let her disappointment sour all the other relationships in her life.

Disappointment sucks. But it's a reality. We are disappointed our relationships never began or didn't endure, but we endure. We are disappointed life didn't turn out as we planned, but we continue to live. If you're feeling disappointed in your ability to direct your own life, it's temporary, unless you choose to make it permanent.

Dealing with disappointment involves either regret or acceptance. Choose regret and you could spend a lot of time living in the past.

VICTORIA'S STORY

· ·

When out socially, at some point in the evening Pat begins to talk about her ex, Don, and what an asshole he is. Pat has been married to her current husband, Jerry, for over 30 years. How many times has poor Jerry had to listen to this story about Pat's former husband? Using every opportunity to slag your former partner is a waste of everybody's time. Continuing to refer to her ex as "the asshole" three decades later shows everyone Pat still has not dealt with her disappointment.

Acceptance may feel impossible now, but it's easier in the long run. How do you accept having to start your life over alone? You focus on what's good about being on your own instead of what annoys you. You decide to fill your mind with what you want out of life instead of how life has done you wrong. You evolve, creating a sense of self that no longer includes that other person.

This is no small task. It takes fortitude. And it does not happen overnight. The old thoughts will continue to crop up. Your goal is to have them crop up less frequently this week than last week until they finally fade into old memories, best forgotten completely.

Forgiveness is often a part of acceptance. You're not forgiving to make the other person feel fine. They don't give two hoots if you forgive them or not. They've already moved on. You're forgiving for your own sanity. As long as you let that person, that old life, dominate your thoughts, you stay in a place that doesn't serve you well. Learn to let go.

BLACK CLOUD DAYS

There will be days that are just horrible. You have to be vigilant about noticing when you start rolling your unhappiness into a snowball of larger and larger proportions. Even in your snotty, tear-sodden state, you can help yourself climb up and out of the morass.

Buddhists call these "black cloud days." Of course you will be sad. There will be days you feel heartbroken. On a black cloud day so much looks bleak and forlorn. No light comes in. And yet if you can notice you are experiencing a black cloud day, you can also tell yourself it will pass. Noticing brings acceptance. "Oh, I'm having a black cloud day and it will pass. But at this moment I feel blue and life feels hard." Having named it, you master it.

GAIL'S STORY
. . . .
On my son's 13th birthday, he was with his father. It was just three months into our separation and this would be the first time I had ever spent a

birthday away from Boyo. I was heartbroken. I wept. And I wept. And I wept. At about four o'clock in the afternoon I'd had all I could take of the day. I crawled into bed and went to sleep. The next morning my daughter said, "Mom, you went to bed early yesterday, even for you." I told her I had had all I could take of the day. She nodded. I sighed. It was a milestone for me. It prepared me for the next Mother's Day, which I would spend without my son. I was okay. And in anticipation of that event, my 15-year-old daughter had the foresight to plan a Mother's Day celebration the weekend before so both my children would be with me to celebrate.

Just as you have to be vigilant about noticing black cloud days, so, too, should you pay particular attention when you have sunny days. When the skies are clear and life is running smoothly, stop and take some time to appreciate the goodness.

Keep checking in with yourself. How do you feel? How does that feeling affect you? Do you want to continue feeling that way or change your thoughts? Can you cycle through the lows more effectively? Getting mired in negativity sucks the life out of you. That doesn't mean you rush through dealing with your emotions. But spend a little time noticing how you feel and deciding what to do about it.

A NOTE ABOUT DEPRESSION

You can deal with sadness on your own, but for depression you will need help. Depression is serious business. It's more than emotional unhappiness; while it can be triggered by emotions, it manifests in the physical.

In the simplest terms, sadness is an emotional response, while depression is rooted in physiology. While the terms are often used interchangeably—people think of sadness and depression as two points on a linear scale—that has led to a lot of confusion in people's minds.

If your mate has died, if your marriage has come to an end, if you feel like your life sucks, you're probably sad. You'll cry. You'll hiss and spit. You'll lose focus and have trouble remembering to do things. Claim your sadness (don't let anyone tell you to "buck up"), because you're entitled. But if anhedonia—the inability to experience pleasure—seems to be your new norm, then you might have moved from sad to depressed.

Everyone will have days they cannot get out of bed, but several days in bed could be a sign of something more than sadness. If you stopped bathing for a day or two, that may be understandable. But if crappy personal hygiene is your new reality, that can be a sign you are depressed.

Depression may affect your sleep cycle, your appetite, and your weight. It will leave you feeling slow and sluggish, restless, angry, irritable, or violent. You may have trouble making small decisions, like what to wear or what to eat. You may have trouble concentrating or remembering things. You may lose a sense of all pleasure—food doesn't have a taste; the world appears grey; you feel flat, numb, or constantly exhausted. Or you may behave dangerously, having reckless sex, driving like a maniac, or gambling.

If you find yourself consuming more alcohol or recreational drugs than usual, you may be depressed. If you feel empty, guilty, or worthless, you may be depressed. If nothing you do makes a difference, you may be depressed. If you have at least five of the following symptoms for most of the day, every day, for at least two weeks, it could be a sign that you should seek help:

- an empty feeling or uncontrollable crying
- no interest in the things that once brought you pleasure
- significant weight loss or gain (more than 5% of your body weight)
- insomnia or inability to wake and deal with normal routines
- irritability, restlessness, or the feeling that you're dragging yourself around
- fatigue or loss of energy, regardless of how much sleep you get
- negative self-talk and self-condemnation
- feelings of worthlessness or guilt
- inability to concentrate, muddy thinking, or indecisiveness
- thoughts of suicide

GAIL'S STORY

• •

I was diagnosed with depression and medicated when I was 18. I had been depressed from the age of 16, but no one noticed. Immigration to Canada and the ensuing "drama" of relocation hid my symptoms. (Adrenalin can do that, which is why some people with depression participate in risky behaviours.) When I tell people I have depression, their first response is usually "No, you're such a happy person!" I'm a walking example of how sadness and depression are two completely different things.

I've had several depressive episodes that resulted in unusual behaviour. I remember sitting at an intersection in my car watching the lights turn green, then red, then green again, unable to proceed because I was trying to decide if I should turn or go straight. The blaring horns barely penetrated my depressive fog. I remember taking my children to school one day, coming home, and sitting on the bottom step trying to decide what to do. The next thing I knew, it was time to go get the kids. And then there was the year I decided to buy seven pairs of black yoga pants and seven black tops so that on any day when it looked like I might get stuck in the closet because I couldn't decide what to wear, I could put on this uniform.

I live with my depression. It is a constant in my life. I'm always on the watch for heightened symptoms. But I'm not a sad person. I laugh easily, I love my life, I'm a happy girl.

While it's been estimated that one in five people will experience some mental health issue in their lifetime, the medical system is woefully bad at identifying and treating depression and its debilitating siblings, like bipolar disorder and anxiety disorder. If you think you might be depressed (or have any other mental illness), you may lack both the energy and the cognitive ability to advocate for yourself. You must arm yourself with an advocate—a lioness—who is prepared to battle on your behalf to get you the help you need. Find someone who understands depression (there are millions of us) and ask for their help in navigating the system. Bring them to appointments with you. Ask them to help make sure you're taking your meds, at least until you come out of the fog.

Depression is hard. I know. But I've survived and I have a good life, and you can too.

SEEKING HELP

Have you heard of the Serenity Prayer? It goes like this: "God, grant me the serenity to accept the things I cannot change, the courage to change the things I can, and the wisdom to know the difference."

GAIL'S STORY

I grew up with the Serenity Prayer because I grew up in an alcoholic household, and it's an integral part of the alcoholic experience. Each time I said this prayer, it made me stop and take a breath. Yes, there are things I can't change. Was this one of them? If this was something I could change, did I have the courage to do the hard thing? And did I have the wisdom to see what was in my control and what wasn't? Just saying the prayer helped to recentre me.

But what if you don't have the wisdom? You have no sense of direction, so the question "What next?" is not even on your radar. If you became single due to an event you did not initiate, your mind may be working at warp speed. If you decided to leave or death was a final release for your mate, you'll still wonder what's next. And if you've come to the conclusion that the rest of your life will be lived in Single Town, you may wonder what that means.

Whenever you deal with change, you use a phenomenal amount of energy to supply your brain. Conscious and subconscious thoughts gobble up your strength and determination. And while you may be exhausted, you may not be able to sleep.

A doctor can help. In times of transition, doctors can prescribe medicine to interrupt the one-track thinking that often dominates late-night wakefulness. A doctor can often give you dispassionate observations about the before-you and the now-you.

Therapists offer another type of assistance, one based on the experience of dealing with other people who have been through what you are going through.

VICTORIA'S STORY
. . . .

A year after my husband died, I went to a therapist. After she listened to me tell my story, she suggested I might never get over this loss. But she said I would find a place to put my grief, a compartment to contain it, as opposed to always having it front and centre in my life. "Right now it aches," she said, "but one day it may become a sweet ache."

If you are circling around and around the same topics, especially things you have no control over, a nudge from a professional might be what you need to get back on the track of life.

THINKING AND FEELING

You may be tempted to push your emotions away and deal with what you're facing logically. It may work for a while, but it usually isn't sustainable. Don't beat yourself up over it. Each of us is a circus. The lion tamer is your intellect, your rational brain, your thinking. The lion is your emotions. You can work on holding yourself together, on taming your lion. But the lion will sometimes break free.

Psychologists have shown that willpower is an exhaustible resource. When you try to control too many things at the same time, you wear yourself out from the inside. You cannot constantly crack the whip on yourself, no matter how much you try.

If you've had to deal with someone who constantly tries your patience, you may have experienced the "snap" of depleted willpower. Ditto if you've had to deal with a child who constantly asks, "Why?" or a colleague who never does as they say they will while you're working on a project together.

Some days the lion will dominate, and some days the lion tamer will rule. Keep reminding yourself that you are doing the best you can and you are learning each day to become the best CEO you can be.

You will change from now until the day you die. Deciding how you want to change is within your power. Choosing to move in the direction that will bring you the most satisfaction is your decision. As CEO of Everything, you get to decide if you'll stay frozen or rebuild your life just as you want it to be.

3 · CHANGES AROUND YOU

Once upon a time people knew the story of your life. Then one day due to illness, accident, separation, or realization, the plot unravelled. The story fell apart. It wasn't the same as yesterday and all the players seemed confused about where to stand, what to say, and how to act.

Over the years social conventions have changed dramatically. With death, the wearing of black full-time was meant to show others your outward grief. People followed rules about how to treat you. People who separated or divorced were talked about in whispers. Now divorce is talked about freely at lunch, and being steadfastly single is *de rigueur*. The rules surrounding being or becoming single are evolving. Are you grieving or planning to throw a party? How do people know what to say?

Some people will amaze you. In trying times they will want to comfort you with food. They will foil your attempts at isolation with calls to say hello, tickets to a play, invitations to go walking. These acts of kindness are meant to show you that you are not alone, that others are thinking of you.

But not everyone will know how to act around your singleness. Even if you've been single for a long time, friends and family may see your singleness as "missing" what it takes to be truly happy. They will see your outside, your words and actions, but wonder what is going on inside you. Your change in status (or your determination to now have a single life) may have a profound effect on them, and they will be looking for signs from you about what to do next. What is your new normal and where do they fit in?

YOUR SHIFTING WORLD

Think of a baby mobile. You know the kind; it's got lots of dangly bits. Touch one piece and the whole mobile shifts. This is what happens to your life when you become single. Your world shifts and so do the satellites around you. The six of you who always played cards together are now five. The four of you who regularly went to dinner are now three. Everyone is trying to figure out how to shuffle the crew so the boat doesn't tip over. If you've declared that you plan to remain just as you are, steadfastly single, your requests to cease and desist the set-ups will shift the baby mobile in people's minds.

Your change in status, or your declaration of singleness, may bring out the best or the worst in others. Some people will project their beliefs onto you. "Oh, you poor dear. How *will* you survive this?" Some people may be jealous of your new freedom. "Why are you still crying? Isn't it great not being stuck doing what someone else wants anymore?" Some may try to wind you into their drama. "My ex is such an ass. I'm still trying to get it all settled. Let me tell you, you're going to have a time of it!"

There's really no explaining why people think or say the things that they do. And you'll drive yourself around the bend trying to make sense of people's behaviour. Don't even try.

VICTORIA'S STORY

A couple we had been friends with for 20 years visited after my husband's death. Imagine my shock when the wife later sent me a letter saying our paths had parted and she would no longer be my friend. That was it! I'd stayed at their home; they'd stayed at mine. We'd vacationed together. I thought it was a deep friendship. And since her husband had been my friend for more than 25 years—longer than she had been in the picture—the loss felt like a betrayal.

Society imposes many labels on people, labels you may not be ready to embrace. But the fact that your status has changed doesn't give anyone the right to label you, speculate on your sexuality, or pass judgment on your attractiveness. They might try to. It will be up to you to manage your response. After all, you are CEO and you manage YOU.

As you embrace your singleness, you might be relishing your independence and wondering why your mated friends keep putting up with the crap they take from their partners. Just as they do not have the right to make assumptions about how miserable you must be now that you are all alone, their status is not your business. And if your friend wants to complain about what an ass said mate is being, your job is to nod, offer support, and let your friend know you'll always listen without judging.

GAIL'S STORY

I can't even begin to count how many people have asked me if I'm dating. They tell me I'm beautiful. They tell me I have so much to offer. They suggest ways of meeting new men because I'm beautiful and I have so much to offer. And when I respond with "No, thanks, I'm not interested in another relationship," they are aghast! What? Have I become cynical? I laugh. I'm so happy I can't believe I've never tried "single" before. But convincing the not-single that I'm just fine with my new reality is almost impossible. So I don't even bother anymore. I just smile and say, "When I meet a man as beautiful as I am, with as much to offer, I'll let you know."

If people ask if you'll partner up, here is the perfect reply: "It depends." "It depends" is such a great go-to answer for lots of snoopy questions about your personal life. "Will you move?" It depends. "Will you have children?" It depends. "Will you cut your hair in a mohawk?" You get the idea.

People in couples may think you're incomplete without a mate. Some folks may pressure you to pair up. Know that it's human nature for like to attract like; your singleness may appear strange to them. Laugh and assure them of your completeness and continue to steer your own course.

ALONE AGAIN, NATURALLY

Emily Carr said, "You come into the world alone and you go out of the world alone, yet it seems to me you are more alone while living than even going and coming." Not surprising words from a woman who spent much of her time painting in remote areas of northern British Columbia. But Emily Carr spoke a truth that resonates for many. If you have uncoupled or if you have determined you are unlikely to couple, alone is a normal state of being. It isn't something to be feared. Nor do you have to accept any stigma that tries to attach itself to you. We come into this world alone. We go out of this world alone. And in between we spend a lot of time alone. And that's okay.

GAIL'S STORY

I never imagined that I would love to live by myself. When my third marriage ended, I reconciled myself to living on my own because I refused to introduce more confusion into my children's already confused life. (I wasn't being totally selfless; I could stand some downtime too.) When the kids left home for university, college, and work, everyone expected me to experience the much-anticipated (and somewhat dreaded) empty-nest syndrome. Sure, the house got quiet, but that wasn't a bad thing. And sure, there was no one to talk to on the daily, but that beat the hell out of fighting or being sniped at. Quiet was okay, I found. And if I needed company, I called a friend, paid a visit, went on an outing. My favourite part of living alone is that no one has an opinion about what I do with my time. If I want to nap, there's no one intimating that's a waste of a beautiful day. If I want to eat slices of Gouda on a fresh Honeycrisp apple for dinner, no one is asking when dinner will be ready. And if I want to stay up all night writing, no one is tapping their fingers and asking when I'll be coming to bed. It's my life and I get to do whatever I damn well please with it.

Imagining being on their own may terrify the people around you. It has nothing to do with you. Your situation simply brings up a sense of dread for your friends because it makes them imagine their own lives in the same context. People avoid you because their uncertainty about your circumstances makes them deeply uncomfortable. Friends say, "I don't know how you do it" or "I couldn't cope." Of course they could. Just as you are reassembling your life, they would too. Unlike you, they just don't know it yet.

VICTORIA'S STORY

Sarah says she gets asked all the time how she copes with living by herself. "Easy. I love my own company. Self-acceptance is a valuable asset. All those people who say they need someone else to make their life complete have lost the plot. Another person is not a precondition to happiness."

If you've always been partnered, there are things about living alone you will have to get used to. The quiet is one. A radio or television playing in the background can help with what may seem like deafening silence at the beginning. Over time you'll need these sounds less as you get used to your own company.

Living alone means it's easy to become isolated, so you'll need to figure out just how much company is enough. Is a walk around the block greeting neighbours enough, or do you need to get involved with a club or an association that meets regularly?

Living alone also means you're on your own if you get sick. If you're used to someone catering to your every whim, or if you need help because you cannot manage on your own, you're going to have to make new plans. Get to know a couple of people in your neighbourhood whom you can count on to pop over if you need help. Find out what resources are available in your community and have those phone numbers handy.

GAIL'S STORY

When Kara turned 40, she realized that she could have an accident in her home and no one would find out for days. "Now I start my mornings with a call to my friend Linda. We both realized that, being single, we needed someone to know if we were okay or not. If Linda doesn't hear from me by 9 a.m. seven days a week, she knows something is up. Sometimes we talk for an hour and a half. Sometimes we talk for 10 minutes. If I didn't have Linda on the other end of that phone I'd feel completely alone."

Pay attention to your health. You can't afford to neglect your teeth, your eyes, your body, since you are now solely dependent on YOU for your care and upkeep. Don't climb ladders alone in the house. Don't take unnecessary chances where you might slip and fall. You've got to think like a single: you are all you have right now, so take care.

IS THERE ANYTHING I CAN DO FOR YOU?

Offers may come to cut the lawn, take your kids for a night, take you out for a drink, walk your dog, do your shopping, or just visit with you, and you should accept. Each invitation will mean one less thing for you to do or think about, especially if you are in mourning over the loss of your mate or the marriage you thought you'd be in forever.

Some people will just jump in.

VICTORIA'S STORY
· ·

Lori and her daughter, Tara, visited me just after Michael died and knew exactly how to help. They brought their work clothes in anticipation of getting dirty. They raked leaves, put away the screens, and tidied up the gardens. They looked around and did what needed doing. And they cooked me dinner too.

Some people will be unfamiliar with how to respond to your loss. They would like to help you but don't know what to say or do. They'll wait for you to signal them that it's okay to step into your life.

It will be frustrating for them (and for you when you look back later) if you don't put an offer of help to good use. But sometimes it's hard to think of what must be done when the offer comes. Time to make a "honey-do" list.

Stick a piece of paper on your fridge and, as a chore occurs to you, put it on the list. Just remembered you have to get an oil change? Put it on the list. Trying to figure out who will shovel the snow or cut the grass? Put it on the list. Need help sorting through your investment portfolio now that everything's changed? Put it on the list. It doesn't matter how large or small the job. Put it on the list. It'll help you to remember what must be done and it'll give you something to point to when anyone says, "How can I help?"

Chores aren't the only things that you'll need help with. Don't be reluctant to ask for support and guidance emotionally too. Be honest about how you're feeling. Ask for what you want. The true friends will help. Those who are only paying lip service will disappear, saving you the trouble of dumping them. Don't take their disappearance as rejection; it is the universe winnowing on your behalf. Be grateful you didn't have to break up with them.

It's sometimes hard to find the words to express what you need, particularly when you're emotionally exhausted. Over time you'll find your own phrases to make conversations easier. Here are a few you can tuck into your repertoire until you come up with your own:

- I need to laugh. Tell me something funny.
- Tell me something good that happened to you.
- Could you lift my spirits? Remind me of the good things in life.
- I know you want to help, but if you could just listen, that would be so great. I don't expect you to solve my problems.
- I know you are worried, but when you keep telling me you are worrying, it makes things worse. I need you to not worry. I am suffering, but my situation is not for you to fret about. I can't worry about you and me right now.
- When you ask me something, I don't know how to answer. Let me think. I'll get back to you.
- Please give me the great gift of letting me express myself.

CEOs learn to be good communicators. People cannot read your mind. If you aren't used to asking for what you want, this could take some practice. Looking into someone's worried eyes as they wonder what to say can be very stressful for both of you. So help them learn how to talk to you. You're 98% the same person, but they don't know that yet. They need your reassurance even as you tell them what you need.

GAIL'S STORY

Brownie and I have a deal. We can tell each other anything, with the explicit understanding that one will not worry about the other. We will each listen. We will often comment. (We love each other, so we don't let anything that's said stick in our craw.) But we will not worry. It's a vital component of being able to vent, to spit and flash, to cry. If Brownie had to worry about me after I told her my shite, I couldn't burden her with it. And the reverse is also true. She set this rule for us. I've learned a lot from it.

If someone attempts the tough-love approach, as in "You're going to have to pull yourself together" or "Don't you think this has gone on long enough?" you may wonder if their attempt to have you "buck up" is in your best interest or theirs. This tactic might, in fact, be their effort to alleviate their feeling of decided discomfort in your presence during this traumatic time. Not everyone is ready to step in and be supportive. Don't let their tough love traumatize you or push you in a direction you don't want to go. If someone persists in talking tough, you might want to think about whether the friendship is working for YOU or not.

LOSING FRIENDS

Have you noticed how people with kids hang out with other people with kids? And people who like tennis gravitate towards other tennis enthusiasts? As your life evolves, you will find that some of the people who have been in your life become like strangers. Life is busy and if you don't share the bonding activities you once did—Thursday-night badminton, Sunday-morning brunch—you need to be prepared for the reality that some friends will drift away.

No matter how close the relationship felt, you may lose friends. Losing any long-standing relationship cuts deeply. You feel banished or shunned. Getting fired as a friend stings. Along with mourning the loss of your partner, now you feel like you're losing another part of your history; it's a double whammy.

Some people may believe you are plotting to take their mates. They imagine you as a mythological siren, calling their partners onto your rocky shores. This may sound funny to you until it happens, and then you'll slap your forehead and say, "Whaaaat?" More often than not, this reaction stems from people's own insecurities about their relationships, not from anything you did. Your becoming single frightens them; it makes them feel vulnerable. And so you are dropped from the party list. A compliment may be taken as a flirtation. An innocent hug may seem overly long to watchful eyes looking for a reason to boot you out of friend camp. Eventually, when people get more comfortable with your singleness, suspicions will subside.

VICTORIA'S STORY

. . . .

I am very careful about how I act around couples. It is intentional because I never want anyone to feel threatened. I am alert to any semblance of impropriety. But despite my efforts, a woman arrived at my home and said, "I have something personal to ask you. Are you sleeping with my husband?" "Christ, no!" I replied, wondering how the hell she'd jumped to that conclusion.

When my friend Lillian became a widow with three kids at 30, and wondered out loud why she was being left out of neighbourhood events, one neighbour set her straight. "You are too pretty. We all worry our spouses will trade us for you."

Psychologists have given a name to this phenomenon. They call it "spousal poaching." Unfortunately, no matter how innocent you may be, others who worry about spousal poaching may see you as a pariah. Time to make some new friends.

As people try to figure out where you fit with your new status, there may be speculation; there may be judgment. Steel yourself. Enjoy a robust dating life? You're a slut. Like your own company? You're a recluse, crazy cat lady, or porn-loving pervert. You can't stop what people think or say. You can only manage how you respond when their judgments come to light. If you can laugh at whatever is said, it'll make people feel foolish and it'll make you look too happy to care.

Some people seem to vanish from your landscape because, as it turns out, they liked your partner better or knew your partner longer. Sometimes friends feel they have to take sides, and history or blood may win. It can be heart-wrenching to hear that your former partner was invited to a party and you were excluded. And you may have friends who try not to take sides and end up on your "bad-friend" list because you actually want them to be on *your* side. They were, after all, *your* friend.

Widowhood and divorce bring changes in places you never imagined they would. Friendship is just one of those places. You can't win people back because they're not prizes. Stop thinking everything is within your control. It's not. The things you can control will keep you busy enough.

VICTORIA'S STORY

Getting fired hurts. When I was fired as a friend, I obsessed about the unfairness. The questions "Why, what did I do?" and "How could a 'friend' say that to me?" rarely left my mind for a month! Finally I stopped berating myself for wasting time on this false friend. Instead I took baby steps. My focus became "dilution." I felt the break in friendship like a stain, something blotting out all the good things. I managed my thoughts, redirecting them away from the hurt, and the stain began fading until one day I forgot to think about it at all.

Once you regain perspective and realize some people in your life will only be temporary friends, you start to breathe

normally. Like all things temporary, they were meant to leave.

You may have a hard time just letting go. You want a final statement, a last attempt at saving the relationship, an acknowledgement that things are over. Whether by email or voicemail—because you can't get a face-to-face—here are some words you can say (or use to frame your own response):

"Hi, I've made a few attempts to get together and talk with you. It hasn't worked out and I'm not sure why. I won't call again. Please know I have always appreciated your friendship and kindness. Bye."

You may not know what is going on with this person; it may have nothing to do with you. This response leaves the door open.

As friends drift away, if you're not prepared to hole up in your bereavement bunker, wringing your hands and sighing, "Poor me," you need to actively work at making new friends.

MAKING NEW FRIENDS

Making friends seemed so much easier when you were a child, didn't it? You just walked up to someone and started playing. Try that as an adult and people will look at you as if you've lost your marbles. Unless, that is, you are part of a group that meets regularly. Within that group, reaching out is natural. So join a book club, get involved with your local curling or base-ball team, take an art class. You won't meet your new BFF by next Thursday, but doing activities you like with other people gives you something to bond over. Then you can extend an invitation to lunch or a local craft show or a movie.

GAIL'S STORY

. . . .

When I separated from my last husband, I knew isolation was going to be an issue because I was also moving to a new town. I knew some of the people who lived there, but I didn't really have a network. So I set out to make friends. I started a once-a-month dinner club, with the first dinner to be at my house, and sent a bunch of invitations out. The idea was to meet once a month, theme the dinner, and have each guest bring a part of the meal AND a friend. I invited five people to the first dinner and we each brought someone else, so we were 12 in all. Someone brought salad, someone brought an appie, someone brought dessert, and there were a couple of side dishes to go with the entree, which (as hostess) I made. We had a great time!

Of course this means you're going to have to step out of your comfort zone. It is so easy to just stay home in sweatpants. Home is safe. The people you already know are safe. But that's no way to expand your horizons, so be brave and step out. Take up a new activity. Try on a new club or organization, such as your local horticultural society if you love to garden, or the Y if you're looking for some exercise.

VICTORIA'S STORY

. . . .

Karla knows how to make friends. When she retired, she moved to a small town to lower her living costs. "You have to give people a chance to get to know you, so I joined the gym. That way I saw the same people each week at the classes and eventually made friends, who I began seeing outside the gym."

Never mind the friends who drop off your radar. As you make the transition to your new reality, surround yourself with nourishing love. You may not be able see some people for a while as you sort through your new normal. If they feel ignored, then they haven't grasped the enormity of the life changes you are experiencing.

GAIL'S STORY

When I was a child, my mother warned me that pushing my hurt, sad, angry feelings down would only make them fester and infect me. She urged me to wrap each bad memory or bad feeling in imaginary tissue paper and tuck it away. From time to time, I was to unwrap the tissue and have another look. She assured me that over time the memory or feeling would become less and less painful and, eventually, I would open up the tissue and what had been wrapped up would have no power over me. I have used this lesson all of my life. I gift it to you.

WHAT ABOUT THE KIDS?

If you think dealing with becoming single is hard for you, imagine what your kids must be thinking. No matter your kids' ages, their worlds will be rocked. And you'll see it reflected in their behaviour, from acting out to complete silence. Even as you're dealing with your own emotional turmoil, prepare yourself to deal with your children's confusion too.

DEATH

When Daddy or Mommy dies, one of a young child's first worries may be that the other parent will disappear too. They may want to sleep with you. They may demand you spend a lot more time with them. They will need your constant reassurance, regardless of whether they are still wearing a onesie or they have a phone permanently plastered to their palm.

Your own grief will take a back seat as you explain what has changed. And you may need some help with this explanation. A grief counsellor can give you tips on the language to use. There are lots of books on the subject. Look for books that cover topics like burial, cremation, and missing someone. Check with your doctor, who may have recommendations for books or other resources. Find a support group in your area or online. Use every bit of help you can get. Your little folk are counting on you.

Be prepared to be asked over and over when the other parent is coming back. The finality of death can be too big for little minds to truly understand. They might not believe it is forever. They might actually forget. Or they may not be able to accept it yet. You cannot lose patience. And as sad as each question makes you, you must steel yourself, smile, and be ready to explain again that Daddy or Mommy isn't coming back.

If you've ever watched a father and son walk down the street and realized they have the same gait, you know what it is to learn by osmosis. Ditto if you've seen a mother and daughter put their hair behind their ear in exactly the same way. Just by being together, parents teach and children learn. There is nothing to replace a father telling his daughter she is smart or a mother telling her son he is handsome. But over time you will want to find a suitable father or mother "substitute" to help fill some of the space left by the missing parent. Encourage a deeper relationship between your son and his uncle or his dad's best friend. Suggest your daughter spend time with an older female cousin. There will always be father–daughter dances and mother–son dinners that make the children miss the departed parent even more unless there is someone willing to step in.

Be open to having several parent substitutes if that works out better. Perhaps Uncle Peter is good at teaching baseball, while friend Jack is better at answering questions surrounding sexual maturing. Maybe your daughter is willing to talk to Aunt Cleo about job choices but finds neighbour Sandy a better sounding board for advice about dating. Fan out the responsibilities so your kids know they are loved, and that many people care for them and are willing to help them.

DIVORCE

You and your mate decided to part ways, but your children won't understand the intricacies of adult relationships and how they can fall apart. They live in a small world and that world just altered dramatically.

In the best of all worlds, you will have joint custody and you will work together to make sure your children's lives run as smoothly as possible. If you have any thoughts at all about using your children to manipulate, punish, or hurt your ex, know that to do so will be to hurt the children in immeasurable ways. Only the most spiteful people use their children as ammunition in their divorce wars.

To better prepare you as you navigate your way through the process of explaining the divorce, here is a quick overview of the typical reactions you can expect from the children.

Up to age 2:

While babies can't put feelings into words, they still absorb the stress of their surroundings. You may be crying more. You may be angry more often. You will definitely be distracted. Watch for changes in your children's eating or sleeping habits. Know that some babies have delayed reactions. If they learned to say "Dada" or "Mama," they may still use these words and look around the room for the missing parent. Until about 18 months, babies don't really form visual images to store in their memory banks. These need to be built. One of you will have custody and the other person should try to see their infant at least twice a week to ensure bonding and to help your child build up a series of images of having both parents around.

Age 3 to 5:

Kids might be more cranky than usual. They may even throw tantrums. Expect resistance to your requests at home and out-bursts in the grocery store. They may regress in potty training, learning to read, or doing what you ask. Reassure them with lots of affection and attention. Kids at this stage are highly imaginative. They may invent an imaginary friend or make up stories about the departed parent or about you. If they say, "Mom drinks beer for breakfast," or "Dad bets on horses," that doesn't mean it's true. Make sure your child knows you are both still their parents, but you now live in different houses and have different lives. While you may not feel like communicating with your former partner concerning your child, you must. At this point your child's needs are paramount.

My parents separated when I was five. I remember one day when my dad picked me up after kindergarten and took me out for lunch. We went to a diner and sat at the counter on twirling chrome stools with red seats. I got to order french fries. When he dropped me off at home, our landlady, Mrs. Rudans, who took care of me after school, was frantic. She'd phoned my mom at work to say I'd gone missing and she had called the police. All because my dad didn't tell my mom what he was doing. My mom was probably scared witless and also mad. There was lots of yelling, and she told me never to do that again and to go to my room. I remember crying on my little bed under the slanted ceiling, repeating, "I want my daddy" as the tears collected in my ears.

Age 6 to 8:

Children are very sensitive at this age and may try to replace the absent parent by taking on their mannerisms. When your daughter is with you, don't be surprised to hear your ex-wife's words coming out of her mouth: "I wonder what we'll have for dinner?" Whenever anything that we like goes missing, it's just human nature to try to replace it. If your ex-husband played the piano, your child may fill the gap of missing sound by banging on the piano keys. Reassure your children that they are not responsible for the divorce and that both parents love them. Let them know things aren't falling apart. Don't keep them in the dark; tell them what's going on so they know where they stand.

Age 9 to 12:

At this age, kids tend to avoid talking about their feelings; they may put on a brave face, appearing happy even as they struggle with the changes. A counsellor may be useful; this may be your first time through the divorce rodeo, but it won't be the counsellor's. Children often express their anger indirectly, complaining about rules and discipline. Whereas they always went to bed at 9 p.m. before, now each night it's a battle. Loyalty conflicts can also pop up; kids want to please both parents and fear they might upset one by showing more affection for and commitment to the other. They already feel divided, so attempt not to react when they bring news of your former partner's new car or new "friend." Under no circumstances should you make your kid your confidant.

VICTORIA'S STORY

When Martha and Jerry got together, he was divorced with kids. The younger ones seemed quite accepting of her, but the eldest, age 12, always looked for a fight. If Martha asked her to clear the table, she would give Martha a long silent stare before eventually getting up and taking the dishes to the kitchen. Of course the younger kids watched her for clues on how to behave. After the eldest let slip a few things that had been said at home, Jerry realized his former spouse had alarmed the kids about money and called Martha names, such as "bimbo." At only 12, Jerry's daughter was absorbing her mother's anger, believing everything she said was true, and making life in her father's house very difficult.

Age 13 to 17:

Teenagers are already a jumble of emotions and contradictions. One minute they want to snuggle up with you on the sofa, and the next they're screaming that you treat them like a baby. Dealing with raging hormones as well as changing patterns in their home life due to divorce can be a nightmare. They may have friends whose parents are divorced but never thought their own parents would do it. They need to understand why you're divorcing. Explain it simply and try to frame it as a "no-fault" separation, regardless of how the divorce came about. If you end up talking about your ex-mate's faults or assigning blame, YOU will be creating a whole other set of problems for yourself. Your teenagers may look like adults, but they are not. Do not treat them as such.

Adult children:

Parents who divorce are sometimes surprised at the response they get from their adult children, ranging from anger to blame to depression. Even adult children can be affected by the dissolution of your relationship. It's great if you and your mate can sit down with your children to explain why you're splitting up and how you will both deal with it, but that's not always possible. You may find yourself on the painful end of a resentful tirade as your adult child struggles to understand why this is happening.

If your adult child is emotionally affected by your divorce, you must make time to listen and explain as best you can. You must reassure them that you will be fine. Playing the "wounded" card with adult children is just as wrong as it is with wee ones. Don't talk about your fury. Don't share your divorce details. Don't complain about your sex life or about what a miserable time you had on a date. Your child is not your mentor, mediator, or mate. Don't expect them to pick sides. And while it might make your heart sing to listen to them slag their other parent, don't encourage it. Time will pass and, unless there is abuse directed at the child, you'll want them to feel close to both their parents.

If a child turns away from you, leave the door open for their return, even if that child is 26 and has lived away from home for several years. While emotions are running hot, don't say or do anything that feels final. Your child loves you. You love your child. If only one of you can remember that, it should be you.

RULES OF ENGAGEMENT

Sometimes being an adult sucks. You find yourself heartbroken and yet you must still look at the person you thought would live with you forever every time you hand off the kids. Even if the split rivalled a boxing match between the heavyweight champions of the world, in front of the kids the tone must be one of quiet diplomacy.

You need clear rules of engagement. Have the conversation about how you will treat each other within earshot of the kids. Discuss what is appropriate to talk about in front of the children when you are together or apart, so you are parenting consistently. Your children have done nothing wrong; they deserve the same parenting you would have given them if you'd stayed together.

Seethe inside, hold imaginary conversations where you always win once you get home, but during the transition from one house to the other, be a picture of calm. Think "Kids First."

Your child's ecstatic response to seeing your ex isn't a betrayal. Delighted screams of "Daddy!" or "Mommy!" will warm your heart if you are on the receiving end, but the person handing off the child may feel like they are being cast aside. While you may feel rejected, that's *your* inner child's response. Do not let that inner child get the better of you.

Your job is to keep your children connected to their other parent. If you punish your former spouse, know that you are really punishing your children, since they must watch you wage war against a person whom they know they come from. They are half Mom and half Dad. You may be angry at your ex-partner, but your children will believe subconsciously that you are angry at them.

Remind your children to call their other parent on birthdays and other special occasions. Out of sight, out of mind happens to kids a lot. They have short attention spans.

VICTORIA'S STORY

Father's Day happens every year, but when Cal's kids got a stepfather, he was there every day and Cal was not. One Father's Day Cal received no calls, no cards, and no presents from his tween and teenage kids. When Cal's wife, Lara, came into the TV room and asked if he was coming to bed, he said, "I'll just wait until 10 in case they call." Lara went to bed and cried, wondering how Cal's kids could forget their dad.

Having primary custody of the children means you get them the majority of the time. But it also means you must be vigilant about ensuring the other parent gets a fair share of the goodies of parenthood.

And let's not forget that grandparents, aunts, uncles, and best friends may have built strong relationships with the children. Your divorce affects them too. So make the effort to ensure those relationships remain strong for your children's sake.

Think about it this way: Did you consider your former mate your friend? Is the way you are treating your ex the way you would treat a friend? Show your kids you can be friendly to people you disagree with. Making the other person look bad makes you look bad and is potentially disastrous for your kids. Be mature. Be clear about boundaries, such as the time for drop-offs and pickups, and the topics that will and won't be discussed in front of the youngsters. Be generous in letting your children receive as much love and affection as possible. That's how you'll help your kids function well through a complicated adjustment.

OTHER PEOPLE'S ADVICE

As you work your way through singlehood, some folks may try to nudge you in one direction or another. Having observed that you are floundering (their judgment), they may try to "set you straight." Friends have ideas—and happily share them with you—about what stage you are at and what you should be doing next. But this is their map of how you should behave and what your life should look like. If it isn't your map, thank them for their loving interest and tell them you'll think about their idea. Push back too hard and they'll get their hackles up. (If you don't care about their hackles, feel free to push.) If you want to maintain their friendship, see their interest (and bossiness) in the light it is intended (love).

There are three things you can do with all that wonderful advice being showered upon you while you are too weak, too distracted, or too distraught to take care of yourself:

1. Accept it. It's a good idea.
2. Reject it. No, thanks. No way. Just wrong. Not my way of dealing with things.
3. Modify it. Take the part that is right for you and graft it onto another part of an idea to make the advice work in your circumstances.

VICTORIA'S STORY

Debbie tried to convince me to move to a certain town. I told her that her suggested location didn't meet my criteria. The next place I moved would be a university town with lots of transportation. But she kept insisting until finally I said, "If you like it so much, why don't you move there?" Debbie said she didn't want to, so I replied, "And neither do I."

When folks try to tell you what you "should" do, keep an open mind. It could be a great idea. While no one likes being someone else's continuous improvement project, sometimes people offer advice that can be helpful. Just remember that YOU really do know what is best for YOU. Sift through the commands and orders to find the information that's useful. As CEO, you know the final decision is yours, so just toss out ideas if they don't work for you.

ALICE DOESN'T LIVE HERE ANYMORE

You have to set the tone for how you'll talk about your dearly departed or your former partner. Others will be looking to you for direction, so you need to address this in a way that makes all of you feel comfortable.

If your partner died, you may want to say how much you miss them. Then say, "It makes me happy to know people still talk about Chris and share their memories with me." Or figure out how to let people know you will not feel comfortable if they mention your partner's name. "Oh, just hearing Chris's name makes my heart feel like it will burst! I'll let you know when my response isn't so raw." Many people will be supersensitive to your feelings, and this is a way to let them know what you need.

If you are divorced or separated, some friends may want to slag your ex, telling you how much better you are to be rid of that anchor. And you might enjoy a little slagging yourself. Just be careful whom you do it with, since people have long memories and bigger mouths. Every CEO will tell you how valuable a reputation is. You want the reputation of being level-headed, fair, and open-hearted.

WHAT'S NEXT?

People will ask lots of questions. Thinking about the most common ones and formulating go-to responses saves you from experiencing that on-the-spot awkwardness. Here are some typical things that might come up along with some ideas about how to reply:

What do you want to do with yourself now? You probably don't know your future plans. It's early days yet. You could scream, "I DON'T KNOW!" out of frustration at being asked this question yet again. But folks just want to be helpful. They want to see you move on. You need to respond in a way that helps them relax and lets them know you'll be okay. "I'm exploring options" is a great reply. Tell them a couple of ideas you're playing with. "I'm thinking of renting out a room." Let them know you are still in the discovery phase; no firm plans exist yet.

How will you ever manage to live on your own? "I've done it before, but if I need help, may I call you?" You've now been given a chance to recruit a helpmate for the future.

How will we play foursome bridge/tennis/whatever with only three? Make it clear that you want to be included. "Maggie is single, too. Let's invite her to partner with me." Suggest ways to get together that are not dependent on your old schema. Movies are great; so is walking or enjoying a local event.

Are you dating? "No, I'm not really focusing on a relationship at this point." You'll want to make it clear that you are not interested in blind dates or being set up, unless of course you are. Friends will try to pair you up. You don't have to play the game. If you want to date, be clear and let people know you are open to the idea.

So, you'll look after (fill in the name) now? "Sure, if I'm available. But I'm not making any firm plans right now, since I'm still getting used to the changes in my life. Call me and I'll let you know if it works." Make it clear that although you're single, that does not mean you're at your friends' and family's beck and call to look after their kids, look after their dog, or look after your aging mother ALL THE TIME. You have a life.

Can you still go to the theatre/golf weekend/spa? "Extend the invitation and I'll let you know if I can afford it or not. Please don't stop asking me to come out and play." Being explicit with your friends reduces their anxiety while you manage expectations. They are free to invite and you are free to accept or decline. No hidden agendas and no dancing around the topic.

So, what's happening with your ex? "I have no idea. I expect that they've moved on, as I have." Don't be surprised if the person then launches into 10 reasons why your relationship was doomed. To cut this off, ask your friend a question about his or her life. "Yeah, that might be true. So, how's your mother doing?"

What do you do with your time now? "You mean, now that I'm on my own and have to do everything? Ha!" Say it with a laugh and then let it go. Folks who know and love you are aware of what you are up to.

As your life shifts, so, too, will your relationships. And so, too, must your expectations. Lunches with individual friends may become *de rigueur* instead of dinners as a foursome. Make sure you have some single friends, or your Saturday nights might be lonely. And know that while some friends may go away, you'll find new ones. Don't desperately cling to what you had because you're afraid of having nothing left. Life evolves. So do friendships. You'll be fine.

The majority of people love you and want to help you. Now that the baby mobile has shifted, all of you are trying out the new reality. Be prepared for some hiccups and some changes. And keep moving forward.

4 · REPLACING MISSING EMPLOYEES

Two people working together can get way more done than one person slogging through a task on their own. That's a given. If you have multiple skills and strengths to draw on, life might seem easier when you're matched. But just because you're on your own doesn't mean life has to be hard. On the contrary, things will only be as hard as you make them. As long as you're prepared to fill in the gaps in your own skill set with the right people, that missing employee (the one you fired, the one who retired, the one who fired you) can be replaced!

GAIL'S STORY

I was the primary cook in our household and my husband was happy to take on the jobs of sous chef and bottle-washer. We were a great team. When we split up, you might think I would miss the cleanup patrol coming in after me. Nope. Not even a little. Our relationship had deteriorated to the point where we could barely stand to be in the same room. So the quiet that came with cleaning up after a meal was more than enough of an offset to the extra steps I had to take.

Part of standing on your own two feet as CEO is figuring out all the tasks you may need help with. First there are the things you cannot do (or do not wish to do) yourself. Cutting the grass, shovelling snow, doing the tax returns, cleaning the house, fixing the dripping faucet. And then there's the *pleasure* you derived from your relationship; that will need to be filled in too.

GET 'ER DUN

When "we" turns into "me," you're going to find that there are a whole bunch of things the other guy did that will now fall to you. It's worth making a list. Know that it won't be a complete list because as crap happens you'll have to decide if you can manage the task or you need to hire it out. But making a list of the things you're most likely to need help with is the first step in identifying the bodies you're going to have to bring on to your team.

VICTORIA'S STORY

Trying to be self-sufficient works up to a point. Taking a dead tree down—well, that's a job a bit beyond my pay grade. When I asked a man I'd hired if he would teach me how to use the chainsaw, he replied in his most manly voice, "Ladies don't work chainsaws." In my case, he is probably right. If you remember the old twirling cards of names and telephone numbers called a Rolodex, you'll get a picture of what you need to compile. For jobs you cannot or will not do, let your fingers do the dialling and keep the names and numbers of these trusted helpers at the ready.

As CEO of Everything, making your team work means being absolutely truthful about your operating style. Think about this for a minute. Are you more likely to do things immediately or wait until the situation reaches mission-critical with sirens blaring? Some folks pay bills as they arrive; others wait until the last minute. Some people get their cars tuned up on a schedule, while others can't see the point until a warning light flashes on their dashboard. Are you a planner or a reactor?

If you are a planner, managing employees will be a snap. If you have always been more reactive, you'll have to work on creating some planning infrastructure or be prepared to be wet, cold, broken, or disappointed when the plumber, furnace guy, mechanic, or hairdresser cannot fit you in until two weeks next Wednesday. While your mate may have been willing to put up with your constant state of crisis, no employee will take that crap for long. You'll end up losing good people to your bad planning.

Part of managing a team is prioritizing what needs to be done and deciding who the best person for the project is. Not everything needs to be dealt with right away. Start by making a list of all the things that must be done. It doesn't matter if those things have to be completed once a week, once a month, or once a year; put them on the list.

If you end up with a list 20 pages long, don't lose heart. It's most important to get the things you need to do out of your head and down on paper so that your brain is left free to think. Once things are all written down, you won't believe how much easier it will be to decide what to do next. All CEOs manage operating divisions, so you might want to sort your service providers by theme: car, finances, home, education, kids.

It's easy to look at a long to-do list and just want to shove it in a drawer because you can't even imagine where you'll start. Don't let yourself become overwhelmed.

Now it's time to prioritize. Put an "A" beside the things that are urgent. Those are things that have a close deadline, things that must be done on the regular, things that will make your life a living hell if you don't deal with them. Think winter snow tires; waiting until it snows means you'll go to the back of the line with all the other non-planners. Finding yourself on February 27 wondering where to put your Registered Retirement Savings Plan (RRSP) money, or if you even have any to contribute, means scrambling to make a decision, which could very well lead to the wrong one. Missing your property taxes by even one day means getting dinged with a penalty charge.

GAIL'S STORY
. . . .

I've had three husbands, and between them I couldn't stitch together a single handyman. I've had girlfriends with husbands who could build or fix anything and—I cannot tell a lie—it sort of made me jealous. But when I divorced, I had no problem with the concept of hiring someone to do work around my house. The instinct came naturally, since I'd had to hire people all through my marriages.

Put a "B" beside things that are important. Those are things that must be done but not immediately. Now you need to decide which important things have priority. Time to number those things in the order in which you plan to do them. Take asking for time off from work. Sure, you're not leaving on vacation for three months, but if you wait too long, by the time you tell your boss which days you want off, someone else may have planned their trip to Cancun and you won't get away to Cuba when you want. And while you know your furnace needs to be serviced annually, if you keep putting it off, it'll become a crisis when it's making a funny sound at 10:30 at night.

Put a "C" beside the "nice to have done" tasks. Nice to clean out the closets. Nice to sort the photographs. If you're like Victoria, you'll keep these things on your list because eventually they must be done and a constant reminder is a motivator. If you're like Gail, you'll cross all these things off your list because she hates too-long lists that never have an end in sight, so she only adds these sorts of tasks to the list in the week she actually plans to take care of them.

Now it's time to decide who will do the things on your list. Some tasks require more experience or expertise than you possess. Time to assign a "ME" or "EMPLOYEE" to each item on your list. Don't worry just yet about who that employee will be.

If you are overwhelmed by the number of MEs on your list, that should tell you something. As Spider-Man's auntie reminded him, "You're not Superman, you know." Go back over your list and decide what you can delegate to employees and what you must actually do yourself.

Look for ways to make your to-do tasks easier if you must tackle them yourself and you're short on time. It is no coincidence that grocery stores now offer a wide selection of prepared meals. Once upon a time if you didn't want to cook, you had to choose frozen pizza, canned soup, or cereal. Today your selection ranges from salads to sushi to roast chicken, all for a price.

GAIL'S STORY

A $10 pre-roasted chicken is always on my grocery list. You can't buy a chicken and roast it for less money, so why not take advantage of the time savings? I take those birds home, slice them up for sandwiches, put them into salads, or eat them straight out of the package with two sides! Throw the bones into the freezer and when you have two or three, boil 'em up for soup stock.

Even if you don't have the resources to hire a personal chef, you still have options. If you hate to cook, you can buy ready-made meals. If you have more money than you know what to do with, you can eat out or order in every day. Or you can play the "poor me" card and wrangle invitations to dinner.

In all likelihood, some combination of cooking from scratch (really, you can't make scrambled eggs?) and prepared meals from the market may be your new normal, with the occasional restaurant meal, takeout, or invitation to a friend's place for dinner. Do a twofer by inviting another single person over for dinner and then go to their house the next time.

You cook one meal and get two meals and two nights of fun with a friend.

Cooking for one fewer person is no real test if you're making dinner for a family. It just means you'll have leftovers for lunch the next day. But learning to cook for one will take some getting used to.

GAIL'S STORY

When I became an empty nester I had to learn not to cook too much at once or I'd end up throwing away perfectly good food. I also had to learn to shop in smaller batches. My girlfriend Jazz and I were talking about this one day and she referred to it as European Shopping. In North America we've gotten used to filling our carts to the brim and then stocking our freezers and larders with heaps of food. But North Americans are also the biggest wasters of food. As soon as Jazz planted the idea of the European Shopping model in my head, my perspective shifted. I had a new model I could use. Now I buy only as much as I'm going to cook in the next two or three days, unless something is a really great price or I'm planning a batch-cook.

Batch-cooking dishes like chili, stew, spaghetti sauce, or soup (or, as Victoria likes to say, "Anything you can eat with a spoon") lets you get a lot of cooking over with at once and stocks your freezer for the days you just don't feel like starting from scratch. Making a batch and sharing with another single person (or three) is a great way to vary what's in your freezer.

Don't be afraid to try new things. If the other guy was the barbecuer in your house, that doesn't mean you can never eat anything barbecued again. You just have to learn how to barbecue.

VICTORIA'S STORY

My husband loved to barbecue, and his first gift to me was a charcoal barbecue. I never learned to cook on it. Eight years after his death, having lived without barbecuing, I bought a small beach barbecue (you know the ones you can just cook a hot dog on). Slowly, very slowly, I learned to barbecue. Finally, a friend urged me to buy a better barbecue, and I learned how to cook sweet potatoes, portobello mushrooms, chicken, and salmon on it. Sure, some burnt pieces formed part of the learning, but my skills improved.

WHERE DOES THE TIME GO?

Time is a crucial element in deciding what to do yourself and what to outsource. As CEO of Everything, you can do it all yourself if you like. Or you may feel that you have to due to financial circumstances. Whether you become single through circumstance or choice, you'll have to learn to balance the budget, take out the garbage, stack firewood, cook meals, and change the water filter.

Here is a lesson about human behaviour that may prove useful to you. For any task, whether it is cleaning your house or saving for retirement, there are two components: ability and motivation.

So the first thing you must ask yourself is "Can I do the task?" Do I possess enough of the knowledge needed? Am I sufficiently skilled? Am I experienced enough?

The second thing you'll want to ask yourself is "Do I want to do it?" Am I willing to put in the time to try to learn how to do something I may not be capable of doing? How much time will it take to build the experience to do the job well? And do I have enough drive to complete the task, or will I let everything else I must do get in the way of finishing it?

You may know how to sew, but do you really want to use your time to make a shirt? While anyone can paint a wall, will you be satisfied with your amateurish result, or will that job become one more thing that distracts you from a happy life?

If you find you are letting certain tasks slide, ask yourself if it is ability or motivation that is stopping you. If it is ability, you have to learn how to do the task. If it is motivation, you need to look at the reasons you're procrastinating. If, in the end, you find that this is not a job you will ever get done, bite the bullet and hire some help.

VICTORIA'S STORY

Denise grew up in a family where she was encouraged to at least try every task. Her father said that even if she got married she still needed to be independent, know how to manage the finances, and keep things working. Denise is the go-to relative for toys labelled "some assembly required." "I've learned how to put together all sorts of things. It carries over so that I can take apart most things in the house and fix them."

A word of warning about receiving help: in the early days of your crisis you are today's candidate for assistance. However, in the very near future, another person will need help and rise to the top of the list. On the conveyor belt of life, everyone gets shuffled along as life-changing events accumulate. Friends and family cannot step in to save you all the time. They have their own lives and families to care for. Be conscious of how often you ask for help. Learn to do things for yourself. It may take a little longer, but it will help you develop new skills. And with that comes the confidence a newly minted CEO needs to keep going.

GAIL'S STORY

I've been very fortunate to have friends willing to do things like install light fixtures, fix my downspouts, and recaulk my door. But there are some things I've learned to do for myself. When my daughter informed me that one of my kitchen cupboard doors had "come off in her hand," I decided I'd fix it myself. The hinge had rotted (did you even know that hinges could rot?), so I bought a new one, along with the screws I'd need. I took off the old hinges and put on the new ones, being careful to line them up with the existing screw holes so I wouldn't have to drill new ones. See how smart I am? Then I tried to reinstall the door. Damn! I'd attached the hinges to the door the wrong way. Off they came again. Next I attached the hinges to the cabinet first. That meant I had to hold the door up with my thigh as I screwed the hinge to the cupboard door. This was clearly a job for two people. But I was one person. And I was determined to put the damn door on! And I did.

A fantastic source for learning how to do things is YouTube. Want to figure out how to fix a running toilet? YouTube it. Want to learn to make sourdough bread? Think you might have carpenter ants? There are thousands of how-tos on YouTube.

GAIL'S STORY

. . . .

When I was learning to knit, I needed to figure out how to use the Kitchener stitch to finish toes on the socks I was making. My cousin Vanessa had taught me this, but my brain had filed it incorrectly and couldn't find the instructions. So off to YouTube I went. I typed "Kitchener stitch" into the search and found short and long videos that showed me how to do it. Way better than calling Vanessa, who would have made unmerciful fun of me for forgetting!

The great thing about learning new CEO skills is you never know where they will lead. You may develop a later-in-life career as a painter, electrician, decorator, or gardener. "Try it—you might like it" is a great motto. And it builds self-confidence and self-reliance.

HIRING EMPLOYEES

For jobs that require two people or for which you do not have the skills or the time, you may be able to get a friend to help you in return for a favour to be named later. But there may come a point when all your favour chits have been used up and it's time to call in a professional.

Friends and family will have hired experts, and a referral to a competent professional beats letting your fingers do the walking. Build a list of reliable helpers for jobs that are beyond your capacity. Learn to ask for referrals from people you know who were satisfied with work they had done. Sitting around waiting for the guy whose name you found on the internet to show up is incredibly frustrating and can be risky. And no competent CEO hires without first checking references.

VICTORIA'S STORY

When Karen's neighbour heard that Karen was being quoted $10,000 to fix a leak in her foundation, he thought something sounded fishy. He knew about buildings. He gave Karen a referral to a contractor who discovered that an interior leak was causing the damage. The problem was fixed for less than $1,000. While many contractors deliver high-quality work and want repeat business, there are some scallywags out there. So someone that comes by referral is like gold.

Research forms part of any CEO's mandate, and now that you're in charge and the decisions are all yours, you'll need to know the lay of the land before you act. Failure to do your research could mean you take the wrong steps, hire the wrong employees, or leave yourself open to being overcharged.

When something in the bathroom springs a leak, it'll be up to you to determine whether to hire a plumber at a hundred bucks an hour, or tap a friend or relative who is handy in exchange for something you have that they want. Keep in mind that while your friend may be handy, there are some tasks best done by those who can work to code. Sure, your pal can wire up a light fixture, but they may not be up to the job of fixing a plumbing problem in a way that stops it from becoming a problem again. So whether you're trading or paying, it's buyer beware.

GAIL'S STORY

I had to have the shower stall in my bathroom changed when I decided to redo the flooring. The person who installed the shower was a friend of a friend who was a very handy fellow. Thing is, he thought he knew what he was doing, so he didn't read the instructions. Turns out, caulking around the inside of the shower stall was a mistake. The water was meant to run down the shower walls and into the pan below. By caulking, he actually created a leak that required me to replace the shower again. Lesson learned.

The barter economy seems tailor-made for single people. If you can sew, knit, compute, drive, cook, clean, weed, paint, or wallpaper, you have something someone else might want. And you can trade that something for the work you need done. Perhaps you can babysit for someone who is willing to shovel the driveway. Maybe you can weed the garden in exchange for an oil change?

Make sure the trade is fair. Don't undervalue what you do and overvalue what the other person does so that you end up "overpaying." Know the worth of what you're offering; make sure it's commensurate with what the other person has provided. Then you'll have a trade partnership that you can call on when either of you needs it.

VICTORIA'S STORY

Things I've learned to say when hiring anyone to help me are: "Is there anything I'm not asking you? If I was your aunt, what would you tell me I need to consider? Anything preventative you would suggest I do?" In other words, I'm asking my helpers to share their expertise beyond just what I've presented as the problem. Many times I've been told things that never crossed my mind and helped me save time and money.

ENDINGS LEAD TO BEGINNINGS

Just as there are specific skills and talents a mate may have brought to a relationship, there are also specific roles that person may have played in your life that are left empty once they're gone. Was your mate your best friend? Was the person you shared a life with your perfect travel companion? And who's going to tell you the truth now that the person you trusted the most isn't in your life anymore?

GAIL'S STORY

When I separated from my last husband, I lost more than a marriage. I lost what I thought of as my future. He had been my best friend. He was the person with whom I was going to spend the rest of my life. I was heartbroken. And I was lost. How was I ever going to replace the joy, the dreams, the sense of completeness?

Unfortunately, the man that I married—the best husband ever—was not the man I left; things had changed dramatically and I had no choice but to go. But what I left behind (not just the man but what we had before all the crap) was like a constant ache, a hole, an emptiness. Who would I see the world with? How would I get rid of all the stuff I needed to dump off my chest? Who would watch my antics with amusement?

My daughter has become my favourite travelling companion. I have a few girlfriends who love me so much that I can tell them anything. And my son is the one who smiles sunshine into my world when I get up to my antics. Do I miss the guy who was once the best husband ever? I do. But the holes in my life have gotten smaller and smaller.

TRAVELLING COMPANION

If you loved to travel as a couple, one day you will want to strike out for foreign lands again. Whether it is a weekend getaway to a city hotel, a stay at a bed and breakfast in the country, or a journey halfway around the world, travel will be different. Sometimes you may want to go it alone. Sometimes you may want companionship. If you're signing up to travel with a buddy, you'd best make sure you're going to complement each other (or at least stay out of each other's way) or your holiday won't be much fun.

Aside from the basics, like making sure you both share a desire to go to the same destination and can afford the trip, you should have some common travel habits and be well aware of each other's limitations.

What is your style of travelling? Some people are five-star all the way. Some want to cut corners to keep costs low. Have this conversation before considering a trip with someone else. Will you share a room or enjoy separate rooms because you need your own space?

GAIL'S STORY

Victoria and I took a driving vacation to see a speaker we both admired, and on the way we shared a room. I warned her that I snored. "Alex says I sound like a train," I said. Victoria informed me the next day that my snoring sounded like purring. "She must like you a lot," said Alex, when I told her, "cos, Mom, you sound like a train!" God bless good friends.

If you are considering sleeping with someone you have never slept with before, talk about the snoring before thinking of the money you will save by sharing a bedroom.

Talk about the routines you have when you go on vacation if this is your first time heading off together. Some things you will want to do together, but some things you may prefer to do apart. Perhaps you enjoy a walk each morning alone. Maybe the other guy likes an afternoon nap. Will you always eat together? Does one of you want to explore a site the other one may have no interest in seeing? Decide from the get-go what will be shared experiences and what you'll do independently.

VICTORIA'S STORY

"Describe your perfect vacation day" is one way I open up the conversation with potential travel partners. It gives me a good idea of their focus. Then I get to talk about my ideal day and goals for the trip. I learned this after travelling with someone who slept much later than me and then took an hour to get ready to go out. "Are you always this cheerful in the morning?" she asked on day one. I'd been up for four hours by then walking the streets of Seattle. I am an early riser and, after the first day, I suggested a new plan where I'd go out and return at about 10:30 to give her time to wake up as she liked.

Being in a foreign city can make people nervous. If you are sharing a room and plan to head out on your own, leave a note to let the other person know where you are and when you'll be back. Independent people are used to the freedom to just go. But keeping your travel partner informed reduces worry and lets the other person plan.

Talk about time. When do you each like to get up and go to sleep? This is especially important if you choose to share accommodations, but it also sets the rhythm of the day and the time you'll spend together. If you like to watch television, will the sound bother the other person? How light a sleeper are each of you? And how regularly do you have to eat?

Talk about your personal routines. Let the other person know if you rise with a smile on your face and begin talking immediately, or if your routine involves getting a cup of tea or coffee and reading quietly for a few minutes: "Please give me 10 minutes alone. I wake up slowly."

Talk about punctuality. Will you be at the departure location two hours early or rush to be the last person on the plane? If you like being there early and your companion is a just-in-time kind of person, negotiate a time in between. Getting on a plane with your stomach churning is not a good beginning to any trip. If all else fails, travel separately to the departure location and be philosophical: if they miss the flight, you'll get a room to yourself!

Talk about your expectations. Before the trip, list the top three things that will make it a fabulous vacation for each of you. Is your plan to be active all day and fall exhausted into bed each night? Will you want to start slow and include some quiet time in the afternoon before heading out for the evening? Is catching every connection with time to spare, seeing certain sights, or trying new food every day important enough to make or break your vacation?

Talk about the money. Decide ahead of time where you want to spend it. Who will pay which bills, or will you split everything 50/50? What if one of you drinks and the other doesn't? Or if one of you wants to stay in a five-star hotel and the other is happy with a no-frills room or bed and breakfast so they have the money for experiences? What trade-offs are you each willing to make? Will you want to see shows, go zip lining, or visit every museum? You will have expectations about a trip, and talking everything through helps you see what the other person envisions happening.

GAIL'S STORY

I have a darling friend whom I love to spend time with. But we could never travel together. She wants to find the cheapest room because she spends barely any time there. I want luxury because I like to have downtime in my room. She has a schedule for everything she will do and see each day of the trip. I like to play loose with the schedule, knowing that I'll do one thing but leaving the rest of my time unplanned. If we ever travelled together, we'd have to have separate rooms and agree to meet up for dinner!

Remember that you are so used to your own habits you'll be unaware of just how much they may bug someone else. How much space will you use up in your shared room? How much time do you spend in the bathroom doing your toilette? If you need an hour in the morning just to do your hair, you better say so, unless you don't mind watching the other person brush their teeth or have a poop.

VICTORIA'S STORY

Cam remembered telling his sister he wanted to see llamas when he grew up. Fast forward 40 years, when his sister saw a travel ad for a tour to South America. She sent it to him with a note that read, "Why not?" Cam was married, but his wife didn't want to travel. His sister had never married and loved to travel. So off they headed and they had a fabulous time.

Some relationships do not survive a trip taken together. Being in the same space for an extended period of time is very different from telephone chats, shared meals, and casual meetings. State your preferences ahead of time to ensure you remain friends after the trip.

CONFIDANT

Now that the person you used to share your more challenging or difficult moments with is gone, you'll need to find new confidants. Discernment is such a valuable CEO skill. You need to pick the right person for this job. A confidant is the intimate companion of your thoughts. You have confidence in this person to both help you and maintain your privacy.

This is the person to whom you'll be able to say, "Are you seeing any mistakes I'm making because I am too caught up in my own world?" This person has to be able and willing to tell you the truth. They have to have your best interest at heart. They must give you straight talk, and they must be able to make you feel completely safe as they do.

If you don't know who you can trust with your deliberations and concerns, find a therapist, who will be impartial and must maintain your confidence. No CEO goes it alone. Everyone needs a counterpoint to ensure the big picture is clear.

If you're suddenly single and your primary confidant is now gone, it may have been many years since you've had to think about how to pick that person to whom you can tell your inner thoughts. Take your time. Who do you think truly has your back?

There may be routines that you associate with your mate. With that person gone from your life, the routines have been abruptly halted, leaving you feeling at a loss. It doesn't have to be that way. You can create new routines, new traditions, to replace the old.

VICTORIA'S STORY

My friend Nancy lives in the U.S. She used to enjoy Bloody Marys on Friday nights with her mate. It signalled that the work week was over. When her husband died, Nancy really missed the ritual. I suggested that any time she wanted to enjoy "happy hour" over the telephone, I would join her. This bridged the loss of her tradition and built a new tradition.

BOSOM BUDDY

You may discover that friends are limited in what they can offer you. In times of crisis, you may discover that a friend with whom you regularly had coffee and shared your life is ONLY your friend for coffee and chit-chat. When things get tough, said friend isn't willing to be your rock. So be it.

Just because a friend isn't your bosom buddy doesn't mean that their friendship is worthless. Having too high an expectation of friendship sometimes leaves you feeling betrayed or unloved. Know that the kind of friendship where you can share everything—the kind of friendship where you can truly count on another—is rare and should be cherished. Not every friend can meet the standard of BFF, no matter how much you want it to be so.

Every CEO hires and fires. It's part of the job. We sometimes think of friends as "forever," but that's not always in our best interest. Look over the friends you've had during your entire life so far. How many people have dropped off your radar? It happens. Maybe you lived in the same neighbourhood, went to school together, or had kids who were pals. When your situations changed, the friendship changed. Perhaps you enjoyed privileges in your previous life that are no longer available. You may have joined a club together, shared an activity together, or travelled together, and those things are no longer in your budget.

If you have someone in your life who is no longer serving you well, it may be time to hand out a pink slip. Most people hang on to these friends out of a sense of loyalty or because they have known them for a long time. But if someone's behaviour or language is hurting you, clearly they don't value you as a friend as much as you value them.

If you're tempted to say to yourself, "I've invested a lot of time in this person," don't. Turning yourself inside out to prove that you didn't waste time or make a bad investment in friendship is a fool's game. Stop looking backwards. It is not about where you have been but about where you want to go next. If the friendship isn't working for *you*, if you are giving more than you're getting, or if the friend seems less friendly, it may be time to ditch the downers and promote more positive people.

When you part ways with friends you will be sad. Yet another gap to fill. But the relief of not having to deal with the stress of regularly interacting with someone who is toxic will far outweigh your sense of loss.

True friendship is a fair and beautiful exchange of energy. You may need to add new friends if you lost former ones or fired friends who were not really contributing to your emotional bottom line. As CEO, you need to get rid of employees who are deadwood, support good employees, and bring in new ones to fill roles that are evolving, even as Me, Inc., evolves.

5 · HELLO, CFO!

If you're thinking, "Oh no, not the money too!" take heart. You've been able to do everything else so far, and you'll be able to handle the money part too. It's not as hard as most people who don't do it think. And the sense of control, of well-being, of self-determination that comes from being in charge of the money is fabulous.

GAIL'S STORY

Donna said it best: "I make my financial and life decisions based on the reality that no one is coming along to solve my financial issues or problems. A lottery win may be more likely than marriage. My perspective is that I need to look after myself."

In many relationships, one person manages the money while the other is happy simply being kept in the loop or ignoring the money completely. If you have been the money manager, there are things you'll have to do to keep things on track as you make the transition to suddenly single. If you've been living in a world where the responsibility for the money has been someone else's job, you've just acquired a new role at Me, Inc.: Chief Financial Officer.

Whether you are on your own or you have family counting on you to keep their lives afloat, you can't stick your head in the sand and hope for the best. You have to be sure that you and your loved ones are safe. There must be money for living now. There must be money for the rainy days everyone encounters. And you'll want to make sure that in your "golden years" you have some gold.

STOP AND BREATHE

It doesn't matter if you've always managed the money or you're picking up the financial reins for the first time; the emotional impact of becoming single will take the wind out of you. You may feel like you are totally incapable of coping. That's just a feeling—just an emotional response—and before you know it, your logical side will step in and take over. But you may need some time to catch your breath, so don't rush things.

10 CFO QUESTIONS

As a way of orienting yourself to your new reality, you need to think about the following questions and then answer them in writing. You may think it's good enough to check them off in your head. It's not. You need to write down your answers. You are untethered right now. Answering these questions for the first time will help you grab on to something tangible as a starting place. As you move through your transition to one-

and-only, revisiting these questions will help you see where you started and the direction in which you're moving:

1. What's your biggest money fear?
2. What do you think about most right now when it comes to your money?
3. What are your sources of income? Is this enough money? If not, what are your options?
4. Who else are you financially responsible for now? In the future (kids, parents)?
5. Describe the lifestyle you have been living in 10 words.
6. Describe the lifestyle you want to have in 10 words.
7. How comfortable are you managing your own money on a day-to-day basis (banking, making purchases)? Where are the holes?
8. How comfortable are you managing your own money when it comes to making it grow? Where are the holes?
9. What are your five most immediate financial issues/ goals?
10. How old are you? If you're still working, when do you plan to retire?

THEN THERE'S THE PAPERWORK

You won't believe how much paperwork is involved in getting separated and divorced or dealing with a death. If you've become single, there will be paperwork you have to gather, paperwork you have to create, and paperwork you have to send out. (So much for a paperless society.) You may feel overwhelmed by all the things you have to deal with, but it's not forever. Brace yourself and work to have the appropriate documents signed, sealed, and delivered properly and promptly.

WIDOWED

There are people who receive an inheritance or an insurance payout and are loath to touch the money. They say things like "It's for the kids," or "It's not really my money," or "My mate wouldn't have approved of me spending money on . . . (fill in the blank)." Some of this is true—yes, some of the money may have been meant to help the children until they can take care of themselves—but most of this thinking is poppycock! Money is just a means of exchange. It has no physical attachment to the person who made it. And it doesn't much care what the person who made it intended you to do with it.

GAIL'S STORY

Natalie was a beautiful woman in her 50s when she was widowed. A friend of a friend asked that I stop in and have a chat with Natalie because she seemed to be struggling over what to do with the money her husband had left her. She and Gregory had planned to retire in 10 years. And then he was gone. And all the dreams were gone with him. Natalie was lucky because Gregory had been a sensible and thoughtful husband who took care to have an estate plan in place and enough insurance for Natalie to see the children through university and beyond. Natalie had no problem giving the kids whatever they asked for using the money their father had left. But she couldn't spend a cent on herself. "Blood money," she called it.

So I asked Natalie, "If Gregory were here today, how happy would he be about how you're doing despite his best efforts to protect you?"

Natalie looked surprised. She thought about it for a moment and then said, "I guess he'd be pretty mad at me for being so silly. He was always such a practical man. I just miss him so much. I can't take pleasure from the money I got because he died."

Do not allow guilt, sadness, fear—any emotion at all—to boss you around when it comes to using the money you inherit or receive as an insurance payout. While it is true that the children have lost a parent, that has nothing to do with the money. It would be disrespectful to your departed spouse not to use the resources they left to create the very best life you can. It's time to gather the reins of your financial life and giddy up!

If you were named as executor (male) or executrix (female) of your mate's estate, your job is to finalize all the paperwork and distributions for your partner's estate. Probating (legally processing) a will is not a small job. Estate law is a provincial affair, so the rules vary by province, but a snapshot of your role as executor will include the following duties:

- Find the will and see if there are any special instructions (like what to do about the funeral).
- Make the funeral arrangements.
- Meet with beneficiaries to determine their financial needs.
- Set up an estate account and freeze any existing accounts.
- Pay the funeral expenses.

- Locate all the documents related to assets owned and debt outstanding.
- Inventory all assets and debts or obligations.
- Notify anyone who may have an interest in the estate.
- Take inventory of the deceased's private and business life.
- Figure out what benefits are due from corporate/ government pension systems.
- Keep the existing assets in order, properly insured, and invested within the limits set out by the law.
- Have real assets (i.e., property) inspected and valued.
- Check for outstanding legal commitments—guaranties, leases, interests in trusts or other people's estates.
- Decide whether to make an RRSP contribution within 60 days of the year of death.
- Pay the probate tax.
- Prepare and file the appropriate income tax returns.
- Sell assets, settle liabilities, obtain tax clearances, and distribute funds to beneficiaries.

The role of executor can be a complicated and exceedingly knotty piece of work that may make you want to pull out your hair and run screaming from the room. That's why you should consider working with a lawyer who specializes in estates to make sure everything that needs to get done gets done. Sure, you can try to do it all yourself if you're determined not to spend a penny on help, but that doesn't make you a smart CFO. A smart CFO knows the value of having an accountant and a lawyer in place to advise on areas where the CFO is not an expert.

VICTORIA'S STORY

Ellen was named executrix for the estates of two relatives who died within a year of each other. OMG. By the time she'd sorted through the houses and belongings, sold things on websites, held garage sales, done all the paperwork, and tried to run her own business at the same time, she was exhausted. It is a big favour to ask someone to be your executor. The valuable lesson Ellen learned was that the time to pare down both household goods and excess paperwork is NOW.

One of the reasons so many people name their spouses and children as executors of their estates is to "keep costs low," which translates into skipping the professional help. Without an accountant, executors might miss eligible deductions and elections on the final tax returns filed. They might even miss filing deadlines, racking up interest costs. They sell assets without getting appraisals and find themselves offside when it comes to investing the estate's assets until distribution. They even sometimes fail to deal with all the debts and taxes owed before paying out money to beneficiaries, which means . . . wait for it . . . they have to pay those taxes or debts from their own pockets!

The easiest estate to wind up is one where all the assets were held jointly or were directed through beneficiary designations. If you and your mate held your home jointly, it automatically (along with any mortgage) becomes yours. Ditto bank accounts and any other assets held jointly. If you were named as beneficiary on your mate's retirement savings plans, insurance, and the like, again, the money will flow directly to you without having to be probated.

An estate that must be probated, that has multiple beneficiaries, or that may be contested because some people don't like what the will says is like a crabby in-law who refuses to go home. You must be patient. You must keep your sense of humour. For heaven's sake, don't try to do it all yourself.

You will need more copies of the death certificate than you imagine. Some banks will even ask you for more than one copy. Begin by asking for 12 and let the funeral home know you may be asking for more. The number of copies you'll need depends on the assets the deceased owned and how many assets need to be transferred into another person's name. If your family car was in your mate's name, you'll need a death certificate to change over the ownership. When you're filing final tax returns you'll have to include a death certificate. And to apply for widow's or children's benefits from the Canada Pension Plan (CPP), you have to have a death certificate. Every time you must legally prove that your mate has died, you'll need that little piece of paper.

If you owned assets jointly, you will have to provide a death certificate to put the asset solely in your name. This could be for a joint chequing account, a house, the deceased's RRSP, or stocks. To collect insurance, you will have to provide a death certificate; if more than one insurance policy was in place, you'll need a death certificate for each. Keep a death certificate in your files because if you decide to remarry, you will need to prove you aren't committing bigamy.

SEPARATED/DIVORCED

If you did the leaving, you probably made some financial decisions before you called it quits. You may have consulted a lawyer. You probably stashed away some money because you knew that support payments or proceeds from the sale of a matrimonial home might take some time to come through.

If you find yourself on the surprise end of single, you may feel like you're running to catch up. Your mate may have been processing (emotionally and intellectually) the demise of the relationship, but it's coming out of the blue for you. So you need to take some time to steady yourself. That being said, there is one process that you should be familiar with so that you know what comes next.

Prior to asking or "petitioning" for divorce, most couples resolve many of the legal issues related to the dissolution of their marriage using a separation agreement or interim court order, which are later incorporated into the final divorce order.

Even if you've managed an amicable separation, you must formalize it with a written separation agreement, particularly when children are involved or when there are significant assets or debts.

GAIL'S STORY

. . . .

I remember being called by a reporter to comment on the unfairness of a situation where a woman was being held accountable for her ex-husband's debts years after the divorce. The woman had never had her name removed from the loan agreement when her husband assumed the debt, so when he declared bankruptcy, the bank saw her as the only recourse for recapturing their money. This is a typical example of how we perceive the divorce itself as the finalization of all connection with the past. That's only true if we've put all the pieces in place for the divorce to be finalized. If you haven't done the work to insulate yourself from your prior partner's indiscretions, consider yourself warned: you'll still be on the hook.

Please, please, do not negotiate your separation agreement sitting at the kitchen table and sign it into effect without getting independent legal advice. And no matter how great you guys get along, no matter how simple the divorce, no matter how far the other guy's bending over to accommodate you, you can't use the same lawyer.

Your divorce advisor (mediator, arbitrator, lawyer) should be working to get you what you need, not punish the other guy. If you get into an adversarial divorce, know that you are giving away money. The average adversarial divorce in Canada costs about $26,000 per person. That's money you could be using to finance the next chapter of your life. And if you try to use your children as battering rams, shame on you! It doesn't matter how angry you are at your ex, your children have the right to a healthy relationship with both their parents.

Keep in mind the two parts of your goal: process and outcome. If you try to squeeze out the maximum outcome (money, custody, house) you want, but the process is soul-sucking and leaves you and your children scarred for life, it simply won't be worth it. Focus on the most beneficial outcome for you and your kids, including a healthy relationship with your former partner.

If, after the involvement of counsellors, mediators, lawyers, and whomever else you have stirred into your divorce mix, the both of you still cannot agree, applications can be made to the court to resolve the issues. Each province and territory has legislation permitting the courts to deal with issues of custody, child support, spousal support, possession of the matrimonial home, and division of property.

The actual Divorce Petition requires a lot of information. You can help your lawyer and save time if you already have that available. See the Divorce Petition Checklist (appendix 1) for the information you should start gathering. You will also need to file a certified copy of your marriage certificate and a certified copy of the Decree Absolute or Divorce Judgment if either of you has gone the divorce route before.

GET ORGANIZED

When you accept the reality that you are the Chief Financial Officer and the only person who truly gives two figs about what happens to your money, it'll be time to get organized. Start by gathering up documents like your investment statements, pension statements, bank account information, credit statements, and insurance policies. You're going to need them to create a net worth statement.

If you feel completely lost at sea when it comes to getting organized and making a financial plan to move forward, hire a professional to help you get started. Do not abdicate your role in the decision-making, but be willing to learn from an expert from whom you can take the reins.

Remember, you'll get what you pay for. When you work with someone who is selling products and earning a commission, you will likely not be charged a fee but will have to buy the products and services sold by that individual/financial company. This usually means a more limited range of options. When you work with a fee-only financial planner, you'll pay an hourly or package fee for the advice you receive. Since they don't make money selling specific products, they should be focused on trying to help you sort out what it is YOU want.

If you hit a body who seems to be pushing you in a direction you don't like or offering options you don't understand, cut your losses in terms of the time invested and move on.

So where do you find this marvellous person who will help you unravel the mysteries of your money? Ask for a referral from a friend, family member, or co-worker. At least you know the recommended advisor has one satisfied customer. Make sure you check their client and professional references.

When you meet, ask where your prospective advisor invests their money. Check to see how their investments are doing. While you aren't going to invest in exactly the same things, you need to know the person walks the talk. If they won't answer you or they hedge, look elsewhere.

Make absolutely sure you understand any product you're interested in before you buy, including the rules and restrictions if you need to get at your money in an emergency. If you can't explain what you're buying to a 12-year-old, you have to ask more questions.

Get the advisor's plan and recommendations in writing before you make a commitment. Regardless of the designations they may have, if they won't put in writing both the strategy and the products they've suggested for implementing the strategy, it's a sign that you can't trust them.

YOUR NET WORTH

One of the best ways to see how you're doing financially is to take a snapshot of where you are at a particular point in time by completing a net worth statement. While your net worth isn't the be-all and end-all of your life—it can't measure your job satisfaction or your overall sense of contentment—it is a great tool for tracking where you've been and where you seem to be going financially.

Grab a pen and a piece of paper. On one side write, "What I Own." On the other write, "What I Owe." List everything. Well, almost everything. Don't bother trying to figure out what your "personal effects" are worth. Since they're not resaleable, you're just trying to pad your net worth statement. And your car isn't worth what you paid for it; it's only worth what someone else would pay you for it, so use the *Black Book* value.

Be vigilant about including everything you owe. That includes your overdraft balance, any "buy now, pay later" programs that have yet to come due, back taxes, and anything you may owe to your RRSP if you used money from it to buy a home or go back to school. Student loans count. Payday advance loans count. And loans from family and friends count.

Be truthful. Be complete. There's nothing like the black and white of the numbers to make you really pay attention.

You'll update your net worth statement to monitor your progress towards your goals because that will help you to stay focused on those goals. Fanatics do updates as often as every month. But you should have a life, so doing a net worth update every six months will suffice. If you need the motivation to keep saving, by all means check how you're doing more often.

To increase your net worth, you need to reduce your debt or increase your assets. This isn't magic. Making this happen might mean implementing lifestyle changes. When you owe money, this weakens your position and leaves you fewer options. The sooner you get your debt paid off, the stronger your financial foundation will be. And the more you allocate to the future in the form of savings, the more rock-solid your future will be.

Don't get smug about the amount of debt you're carrying because your investment portfolio has done particularly well or your home has appreciated significantly. These are things you have almost no control over and cannot rely on. For while markets go down—remember the 2008 stock market correction dragged net worth down—debt doesn't just disappear.

VICTORIA'S STORY

When Matthew lost his job, he decided to just stay in his home until the bank foreclosed. He had put very little money down when he bought the house and hadn't had time to build any equity. He stopped making mortgage payments. He got notices and calls, but eventually the bank began the court process. One day the sheriff came to his house and legally repossessed it. Matthew's credit rating took a severe pounding, making it harder for him to get credit in the future.

If you are counting on your home continuing to appreciate or your portfolio increasing in value as justification for walking around with a boatload of debt, you are travelling

a dangerous road. How would you manage if your home or investments declined in value? If your only plan is based on these two fluctuating markets continually rising, you are basically crossing your fingers.

While money in the bank may not be sexy, it provides peace of mind. And it's there when you need it most. That's why an emergency fund (EF) is so important. Now that you've faced one of the biggest emergencies life can throw at you, you should know how important your EF really is. And now that you are CFO, you'd better make sure you have one in place.

GAIL'S STORY

. . . .

When my last marriage fell apart, I was forced to move quickly. I signed my separation agreement and then immediately put in an offer on a house in the town where I was moving with the kids. (My matrimonial home was in the country and would not sell for a whole year.) I needed to pay movers. I needed to buy some stuff for the new place, like a bed, a fridge, a stove, and a washer and dryer. And, of course, there was the down payment on the new place. (Renting wasn't an option because of my location and the speed with which we had to move.) If I had not had my big, fat, F-U Account—CASH IN THE BANK—I would not have been able to do all I had to do in the 30 days I had to do it.

YOUR CREDIT REPORT

Get a copy of your credit report. It contains information about how promptly you've paid bills, along with all the yucky stuff like collections, judgments, and bankruptcies.

GAIL'S STORY

Tanya was turned down for a loan. She couldn't understand why. She was diligent with her payments and had not overcommitted herself. When she checked her credit bureau, it turned out that the file had combined her information with someone else's. It took her weeks to get the two files disentangled.

Send a written request to one of the two major credit bureaus in Canada: Equifax Canada, Inc. or TransUnion of Canada, Inc. More information can be found online at www.equifax.ca and www.transunion.ca. There is no charge for this service if you ask for your record by mail. If you're into instant gratification, you'll have to pay a fee.

If you question an item on the file, the credit bureau will investigate on your behalf to verify the status of the entry. If an error is found, the credit bureau will fix it and send copies of the updated file to credit grantors upon request.

VICTORIA'S STORY

One year when I got my report I found an item related to a house I'd made an offer on but did not buy. There was a line on the credit report saying I lived there. Wrong. It took me a few weeks to get it cleaned up.

Financial scams abound and if you are single, you're on a scammer's most wanted list. Guard your credit identity by monitoring your credit bureau file at least once a year.

If your spouse had debt in their name and you did not sign for it, it is not your problem, no matter how many people phone you and try to weasel the money from you. Whichever bank, credit card, or loan company made the loan must absorb the loss. They will try to get the money from you, perhaps even using words designed to hurt or make you feel guilty. Tell 'em to take a hike.

If your spouse had debt that you did sign for, you must make sure your name is removed from the loan documentation as part of your separation agreement, or you will continue to be liable for that debt, regardless of what you and your ex agreed to. Banks don't care what your deal was. They only care about names on the file. Get yours off!

In appendix 2 you'll find a checklist you can use to make sure you inform everyone who needs to know of your change in status.

KEEP THE WHEELS TURNING

CFOs have to keep the wheels turning through good times and bad. As the guy in charge, you will be responsible for making sure your financial life doesn't go to rack and ruin. While you may need to take a time out emotionally to deal with the demise of your life as you once knew it, the bills still have to be paid if you want to keep the lights on.

GET OVERDRAFT PROTECTION

When you're in a transition, overdraft (OD) protection beats the pants off non-sufficient funds (NSF) fees and the bruise on your credit report because you were distracted. Just make sure you buy the right plan.

Don't confuse the kind of overdraft protection you "buy," for which you sign an agreement, with what some banks call "bounce protection" or "courtesy overdraft protection," which they offer to save you from the embarrassment or hassle of a returned cheque. The latter can be very expensive.

GAIL'S STORY

A woman wrote me to say that she was appalled when her bank statement came in and she had over $160 in bounce fees. While the average courtesy overdraft fee runs to about $29 a month, the fees can be substantially higher depending on how undisciplined you are. And since the fee is levied regardless of the amount you go into overdraft for, it can be astronomical when you calculate it as a percentage of the "loan," which is exactly what this woman discovered.

Some banks make their OD protection even more profitable by charging up to $5 for every business day an overdraft is created or increased. So if you go into overdraft on the 12th, you'll be dinged with a $5 charge. Buy something for a-buck-twenty-five the next day and go further into your overdraft and you'll be dinged with another $5 fee. Ouch!

Make sure you've signed up for the traditional overdraft protection, for which you sign an agreement, so you know what you'll pay in interest, and for which you pay a flat monthly fee. Do NOT fall into the trap of thinking that overdraft protection gives you a licence to ignore your cash management. Overdraft protection is a temporary solution to the potential problems that may arise because you're in flux and aren't thinking completely straight. It is not a licence to spend whatever you want whenever you want. And you're not allowed to live in overdraft, squeaking into the black when your paycheque passes through your account. Overdraft protection is for the short term. In about six months, you should get rid of it because you're back to thinking straight and managing your cash flow.

BUDGETING

If you've never budgeted before, you're going to learn to now. Why people fear or hate budgets boggles the mind. A budget is simply a plan for how you'll use your money, allowing you to sort out where you want to allocate your resources. Budgets aren't tight or loose, like a pair of shoes. They are a record of where you put money in the past and a plan for where you want it to go in the future. Money doesn't spend itself; you do.

CFOs are the stewards of a company's resources. Whether the company is large and rich, or small and with limited resources, the CFO runs the financial show. As CFO your goal is to meet the majority of your requirements with the least amount of your resources so that you have some to sock away for the future.

If you've never had to account for how you've used money because the other guy did all the heavy lifting when it came to managing it, your new role as CFO will take some getting used to. Think about how much self-control you have. Think about how disciplined you are. Now that you're CFO and in charge, you're going to act like a grown-up. You can no longer afford to live only in the moment; you are now responsible for your future. (There will be more about this idea of balancing today's needs with future ones when you get to a later section in this chapter, "Managing Your Resources.")

It's time to figure out where you'll be getting your money to live and how you will use that money to your best advantage. Yup, it's time to make a budget.

(If you've never made a budget and have no idea where to even start, get a copy of *Debt-Free Forever* and work through the process outlined there.)

One of the things that will likely be top of mind is replacing at least some of the extra income you had when you were paired. Make sure you account for all the money you'll be entitled to receive so you can make a realistic budget. Here is a list of typical sources of income so you don't forget anything in your planning:

- Salary
- Rental property income
- Business income
- Private pension (from an employer)
- Private pension spousal payout (from an employer)
- Investment income (interest/dividends)
- Canada Pension Plan (CPP)
- Canada Pension Plan Survivor Benefits (check with Service Canada)
- Old Age Security (OAS)
- Guaranteed Income Supplement
- Spousal support
- Child support

- CPP children's benefits
- GST/HST credit
- Other social assistance income (e.g., Ontario Disability Support Program)
- Employment Insurance benefits
- Federal family benefits
- Provincial refundable tax credits
- Workers' Compensation benefits

A special word about child support and spousal support payments: It is a sad reality that there are parents who refuse to support their families even after the courts have ordered them to pay. Nearly two-thirds of support orders in Canada are in arrears. Sometimes it's a case of not being responsible. Sometimes it's a case where well-meaning parents find their personal circumstances have changed and they simply cannot keep up with support payments.

As CFO, it's your job to make sure the whole family isn't thrown into a tailspin when a support cheque does not arrive. That means creating a budget that does not depend on the support payment.

If that sounds crazy to you, look at the statistics and you'll soon see it's the smart thing to do. Build your must-have budget without the support payments and then use the payments to supplement your must-haves. In other words, don't count on the support payments for rent or food. Use them instead for things like clothing, adding to your emergency fund, and extracurricular activities. If a cheque doesn't arrive when you expect it, your whole budget won't blow up.

When it comes to the expenses on your budget, there are the standards like food and clothes, entertainment, and transportation. But budget expenses are as varied as the people making budgets. Will you have to pay utilities, or are they included in your rent? Do you have to buy trash tags, or is garbage in your community collected without an additional charge? Do your children play sports? Do you own a car? Are you giving your children an allowance? Do you wear glasses?

The best way to decide what needs to go into your budget is to look at how you've been spending your money in the past. A spending analysis looks at the past six months to see where the money went. That'll give you the categories you need for your budget.

Keep in mind that you may lose the benefits your partner received. Benefits typically expire, and you need to know the expiry date so you can budget those expenses into your own spending plan.

FIX WHAT ISN'T WORKING

If when you do your budget you find that more money is going out than coming in, as a responsible CFO you have to do the hard thing: cut costs. And you have to tell your board members (your family) just how this will impact them. Some expenses will be easy to cut. Eliminating things like premium cable (or all cable), fancy phone features, out-of-home meals, newspaper and magazine subscriptions, and your morning coffee on the way to work will be no-brainers. Slicing back on kids' activities will be harder. But you can't spend more money than you bring in, so cut you must.

In some circumstances you may even find you cannot afford to live independently. Before you throw your hand to your forehead and fall away in a dead swoon, remember you lived with people before and it didn't kill you. Sharing accommodation may turn out to be the best thing in the world for you. Or it may be horrible until you find the people you can live with. But if your options are to live with someone else or go into debt, know that the debt will eventually catch up with you and your life will be even more horrible when it does.

Your debt levels may be causing some strain on your cash flow: all those payments really cramp your style, don't they? It may take a Herculean effort to get rid of your debt, but it will be worth it.

(Once again, if you've never made a debt repayment plan and have no idea where to even start, again, get a copy of *Debt-Free Forever* and work through the process outlined.)

If you don't have an emergency fund, you need to establish one. If you haven't saved anything for your future, it's time to get busy now that you know you're the only one who will be supporting you over the long haul. And if you haven't set aside a penny for the kids' post-secondary schooling, you'll want to look into that too.

If you choose not to make the difficult decisions, sometimes they will be made for you. This is the least desirable outcome for any CFO. Dig in your heels and decide you don't have to change your lifestyle despite the change in your circumstance, and your creditors will become the boss of you. Skip paying your utility bills on time and you'll end up living in a cold, dark home. Use shopping as your emotional salve and you'll become a financial slave to the credit card company, working extra hours to pay all the interest. Or decide you're going to be in control, you're going to make the decisions that impact your life, and you can make your new reality what you want it to be.

You may be CFO for three months, three years, or a lifetime. You'll grow into the position and, happily, cannot unlearn being in charge. At first every decision may feel difficult and take up a lot of your time. You may consciously plan, write lists, check numbers. Eventually, the decision-making becomes more familiar, almost second nature. You change because you're able to see a more connected picture. And as you change, you realize that being CFO, being the guy who knows what's going on with the money, is a good thing.

FEAR MAKES FOR BAD CHOICES

Loads of people harbour the fear of becoming a bag lady or a homeless dude. When there's been a significant change in your circumstances, and your brain decides to play through all the worst-case scenarios it can come up with, bag lady or homeless dude may be one of those scenarios.

In reality, few people become destitute. You are strong and capable—you may simply not remember just how strong and capable given your current emotional state. If you let fear undermine your confidence, you'll make bad decisions (something else to beat yourself up over) and the cycle will continue because an anxious brain is less equipped to handle uncertainty and complexity.

If you make a mistake, own it and move on. In the investment world there's an adage: "Your first loss is your best loss." That first loss really makes you sit up and pay attention. It makes you learn what to do (or not do) the next time. And it sets some parameters for what's truly important to you. So learn from your mistake and keep moving forward.

MOVING FORWARD

Your plan for life has changed. No doubt it will change again. The way to cope with your potential futures is to spend a little time thinking about what you would do if . . .

CEOs and CFOs have to be strategic planners, and they call this "what if" planning. They routinely imagine various scenarios and how they would react so their company would survive.

Below are some things you might want to think about so that, if a change in strategic direction becomes necessary, you're not completely unprepared.

If you're tempted to think of this as a waste of effort and time, know that this is the kind of discipline that leads to success. Being prepared for potential outcomes is what separates those who manage change well from those who moan, "I never saw *that* coming."

GAIL'S STORY

• •

Sometimes it takes people a little longer to get to the planning they need to do to create a strong personal economy and a secure future. Joanne told me she knew she'd waited a little too long. "At 52 I look ahead to see what I have to do in the next 15 years, questions I should have been posing 15 years ago, to make sure I'll be okay. So now I'm thinking about other ways of being in the world that don't involve living by myself. I look at co-housing models and wonder if I'll end up sharing with friends or siblings. If that doesn't happen, what else can I do to look after myself in my old age? I'm pretty cold-eyed about when that's going to happen. I'm not attached to staying in my house, worrying about a roof, and shovelling snow at 85. I see myself moving into an apartment because I don't want the responsibility of a house. If anything goes wrong, I want to phone a number so someone can come and look after it."

IF YOU HAVE KIDS STILL LIVING AT HOME:

- Can you afford to stay there?
- Can you remain in the neighbourhood so the kids can stay at the same school?
- If you must move, what would be your preferred location?
- Can a relative provide a temporary home while you get back on your feet?
- Would you move for financial or emotional reasons?
- Do you want to retain "normalcy" or make a fresh start?

IF YOU WILL BE LIVING ALONE:

- Can you afford to keep your current home or must you downsize?
- Can you rent rooms?
- Would selling your home and renting give you more financial freedom?

- Will you move to an apartment, a condo, or a smaller house?
- Can you move in with a friend or relative to cut costs?

IF YOU EXPERIENCE A SERIOUS HEALTH ISSUE:
- Will you hire a nurse?
- Do you have family or friends who could be your caregivers?
- Do you have powers of attorney for personal care in place?
- Do you have insurance to cover your costs?
- Do your caregivers know how to access any health benefits provided by your workplace?

IF YOU FIND A NEW MATE:
- Will you cohabit or "live apart together," keeping your separate spaces?
- Will you move or will your new partner move in with you?
- Will you join forces financially?
- Will you write a pre-nuptial (or co-habitation) agreement?
- Will you buy a home together?
- How will you protect your children's interests in your assets?

IF YOU LOSE YOUR JOB:
- How much savings do you have and how long will they last?
- How ready do you feel to hunt for a new job?
- Are there many other similar jobs in your area?

- Would you need to change locations to find a job?
- How up-to-date is your network of contacts?
- How up-to-date is your resumé?

IF YOUR AGING PARENT NEEDS YOUR SUPPORT:
- Do you have a place for them in your home?
- Do they have cash reserves to pay for care?
- What can other siblings/family members do to help?
- Are there any government services available to help?

IF YOUR CHILD NEEDS YOUR SUPPORT:
- Will your support keep them dependent or contribute to their independence?
- Did they make a mistake they need to learn from or is this a genuine emergency?
- What agreements will you come to regarding repayment/reciprocity?
- Can you afford to support them?

WHEN SPOUSAL SUPPORT STOPS:
- How much money will you need to replace?
- Have you made yourself ready for the job market?
- Have you explored options for either reducing costs or increasing income?

WHEN THE CHILD SUPPORT STOPS:
- Have you redone your budget without the support payments to identify any shortfall?
- Have you discussed the end of support with your child

to make it clear things are changing?

- Have you identified expenses your child must assume (car insurance, cellphone bills, school tuition)?
- Have you explored options for either reducing costs or increasing income?

IF YOU MUST RETIRE EARLY:

- If you have a company pension plan, is there a provision for early retirement?
- How soon can you access government benefits? How much will you get?
- What are your fixed costs? What are your variable costs, and can you trim them?
- Are there other jobs you could do to fill in some of the income lost?

WHEN YOU FINALLY RETIRE:

- Have you made a retirement budget and practised living on it in preparation for retirement?
- Will you get another job for either income or fulfilment?
- Have you eliminated/reduced costs associated with working, such as memberships or auto-related expenses?
- Have you planned for rising costs during retirement?

WHEN YOU DIE:

- Do people know how to contact your family and friends?
- Do people know where your will is and who your lawyer is?

- Have you got all your financial paperwork in order so it is easy for the executor to take care of your estate?
- Have you prepared a list of passwords to access accounts? Who did you give it to?
- Do people know what to do with your pet?
- Have you prepaid your funeral? Where are your funeral instructions?

UPDATE EVERYTHING

A change in status means just about every piece of legal paperwork must be updated. While tending to the paperwork may not be the first thing on your mind as you struggle to put some semblance of normalcy back into your life, getting past the six-month mark without making the necessary changes means you're procrastinating. You have some time to breathe; too much time means you're in denial. Get busy!

Your Will. If you have one, it needs to be changed because your status has changed. If you don't have one, make one. Don't want to spend the money? Don't think it's really a big deal? Go and type "dying without a will in Canada" into Google for the scary details of what a mess you will leave behind for your loved ones. If you love your family, if you don't want the government to take more than its fair share, make a will.

Your Personal Care Power of Attorney. If something happens and you are unable to make medical decisions for yourself, your family cannot simply step in and do so for you. They need your permission. No one wants to think about becoming a drooling fool, but you'll save your loved ones a lot of guessing and grief if you make it clear what you want and who can make the big decisions for you by completing a personal care POA.

VICTORIA'S STORY

A few years ago I created a list for my family and friends. It included the names and details of my lawyer, doctor, and banker, and the locations where my will, powers of attorney, and accounts were held. It also included the names and contact details of my close friends in different cities. I sent the list to everyone so that if I ever could not be reached, they would have someone to call to come over to ensure I was still alive. And if I was in dire circumstances, my neighbours would know how to contact my family. When you are single, you take precautions.

Your Financial Power of Attorney. This document identifies who will take care of your finances (your home, your possessions, all your assets) if you are unable to make decisions for yourself because of physical or mental incapacity. Make sure this person will know how to access your accounts, especially if you suddenly become unable to communicate.

Your Insurance Policy. Change the beneficiaries on your existing policies so the money can pass directly to whom you want and avoid probate fees. While you're at it, chat with an insurance broker to make sure you have enough and the right type of insurance now that you are on your own. If you have children who are dependent on child support, insist on an irrevocable insurance policy payable to your children in the event of a supporting ex-spouse's early demise.

Your Work Benefits. People don't always think about benefits, but without them one event can completely disrupt a budget. Think $2,000 for dental work or $600 for physiotherapy. Will your former spouse's benefits cover the children's medical needs? For how long? Is there a time limit to when you are still covered by your former spouse's plan? Do you have work benefits you should now put in place? Do you need to buy medical insurance?

Your Pension Plan at Work. Most people look at their retirement savings only as they approach retirement. Look at your plan now! Is it a defined benefit or a defined contribution plan? If you don't understand the difference, ask your human resources department to explain it to you. What will you receive at retirement? Will it be enough? Can you do anything to maximize your pension? Is it better to put extra money into an RRSP or a Tax-Free Savings Account (TFSA)? Where will you find the extra money to save?

Your RRSP/RRIF/TFSA. Change the beneficiaries for all your registered plans. If you don't know whom to name, make it your estate for now and plan to review this again in a few months. In the best of worlds, you will name beneficiaries directly so this money doesn't have to be probated and your beneficiaries can save on probate fees.

Your Name. If you've decided to revert to your maiden name, you'll need to show your Canadian birth certificate or citizenship papers along with your court-issued divorce order to get your government ID updated. Get your driver's licence updated first. That'll make it easier to change your name everywhere else. Update all your accounts, identification, and memberships at the same time.

GAIL'S STORY

When I separated from my third husband, I applied for new bank accounts and credit cards under Vaz-Oxlade (after using my married name for 18 years). I was furious and could only think of distancing myself from my husband. But I didn't change my driver's licence or my passport because I hadn't yet divorced and I didn't want complications when travelling with my children. I vacillated between names for a long time. Now, when I go into places and they look me up on their computers, I have to go through an array of names. Sometimes I feel like, "Well, it's Tuesday, so I must be Gail Vaz-Oxlade." Don't do it this way!

MANAGING YOUR RESOURCES

Becoming CFO means recognizing that if you don't manage your resources, no one will. Those resources—whether they come in the form of insurance benefits or other kinds of inheritance, matrimonial settlements, ongoing payments from (government or private) pension or support orders, or the sweat of your brow—are finite. Managed badly, they will be gone and you will be broke. Managed well, you'll have money now and money later.

GAIL'S STORY

Cameron has been single forever. There have been relationships but nothing's ever stuck. As we were sitting around chatting with friends, some people were saying how much easier it is for couples who have each other as backups. I disagreed. And I was surprised when Cameron did too. "I look at my parents—two good incomes and my father spent it all. My mother would have been 100% better off on her own financially. I have faced different financial challenges. When I lost my last job I didn't realize it would take me two years to get my income back on track. But all kinds of people have to recover from difficult financial times. I've watched friends get divorced at 45 and it's been a financial train wreck. So everyone goes through challenges. I'm glad I was the only one I had to consider before I made big financial decisions like selling my house to pay off all that debt I racked up when I was unemployed."

MONEY NOW, MONEY LATER

You may have money that falls into two distinctly different pools: lump-sum amounts and ongoing amounts. If, for example, you receive an insurance payout upon the death of your mate, that lump-sum amount must take care of some of today's needs and much more of tomorrow's. Ditto a matrimonial settlement from, say, the sale of a home. You may also have ongoing income that must be matched against your ongoing expenses so that, in the end, there's a little something left over to save for the future.

If you know you'll be getting a lump sum of money, open up a new banking account for that money, since money lumped into your normal accounts may lose its "specialness." In business there is a distinction between "capital expenses"—money to buy things like a car or an education—and "operating expenses"—money to carry on the workings of life, like food and repairs. Keep your new stash of cash separate until you decide how you plan to use the money.

You only have a set amount of time during which to make money and, if you plan to last well past your working life, you're going to have to figure out what the balance should be between today's wants and tomorrow's needs.

Getting a lump sum of money may make you feel rich. Whether it comes as an insurance payout or a divorce settlement, a cheque for $200,000, $500,000, or $1,000,000 may seem like a lot of money. Feeling flush opens you up to all kinds of temptations. How could you ever use it all up?

GAIL'S STORY

When Patti showed up on my doorstep holding her ex-husband's settlement cheque for $325,000, she said, "Here, you take this. If I keep it I'll spend it. I need you to make sure it lasts me a long time." No way was I taking on that job. Mixing money management and friendship is a recipe for no friends. Instead I sat Miss Patti down and we talked about what she wanted to do with the money, how long it had to last, and where she would put it so it earned a little sumthin' sumthin' without keeping her up at night. She left my house as weepy as she had arrived, but this time it was because she was so relieved to have a plan, not because she was so afraid she was going to blow the money!

It's easy to think a lump sum of money will last forever, but if you spend $40,000 of your stash a year, $200,000 will last

only five years. Whoosh! What was that? That was your stash of cash—now it's gone and you'll have to get used to living on a lot less. You won't believe how easy it is to blow through money if you're not being vigilant. Witness all the lottery winners who are dead broke just a few years after receiving more money than anyone in their right mind could spend.

While being too overwhelmed by your new life to cook at the end of a long day may feel like justification to eat out or order in, developing a restaurant habit has its consequences. It's much the same when it comes to choosing where you will live. It's become *de rigueur* to want a home equipped with every conceivable convenience. That condo with marble in the front hall and granite in the kitchen is lovely. That house with the bathroom that's more like a spa is nice too. But if you're spending so much on your mortgage that you don't save a cent for the next chapter of your life, you're going to run into trouble. Better to opt for a simpler existence with money left over for important things down the road, like heat and food.

VICTORIA'S STORY

When Bob took early retirement from a utility company, he was offered a choice between a lump sum and an ongoing pension. His wife, Karen, nearly choked at the meeting when she realized that the lump sum would be $1.5 million. She wanted the lump sum. With his family's history of early death, Bob also favoured that choice. They took the money.

When Karen asked my opinion, I said to roll as much of the lump sum as possible into Bob's RRSP so they'd have money at retirement. But the idea of all that money addled their brains. They took the sum in cash, which meant they hit the top tax bracket that year, paying over $500,000 in taxes. While they felt like they'd won the lottery, it was really the government that had won! Bob and Karen bought a commercial building for her business and a recreational vehicle that was the equivalent of a house on wheels, went on a cruise, and put in a pool. And when retirement rolls around? Well, they will have a decade's worth of memories to keep them warm while they learn to live on the $36,000 in government benefits they'll likely receive.

Balancing today's wants with tomorrow's needs does take a little thought and some planning. Maybe a little less itch-scratching. If you aren't of a mind to conserve, what are you planning to eat when your earning days are at an end and you're left with a lot of stuff but not much money? And how much of that stuff can you burn to stay warm?

If you're one of the Joes singing, "Well, I'll just go back to work or keep working," what will you do if that's not an option? What if a medical condition stops you from working? How about if there are no jobs you can do? Going back to work isn't always an option.

ALLOCATING A LUMP-SUM PAYOUT

Initially, do nothing with whatever lump-sum money flows into your hot little hands. Let the experience settle before you make any decisions. And if people ask you to take a particular action, to share your bounty, or to let them help you invest, say, "Let me think about it," and put some space and thought between you and the decision.

What you end up doing with a lump-sum payout is largely dependent on your specific financial situation.

If you have consumer debt (anything other than a car loan, mortgage, or student loan), getting rid of that debt should be a priority, since you'll want to limit the amount you pay in interest and free up cash flow for your living expenses.

If you have no emergency fund, set some money aside for the crap that life brings. (Being in the midst of said crap, you should see how important an emergency fund will be down the road.)

If you have no income—you're going to have to get a job, but you'll need a few months' cash flow until you do—allocate just enough from your lump-sum payout to cover your most basic needs. If you're fulfilling all your wants with your stash of cash, your motivation to get off your duff and get a job will be way lower than if you find yourself eating soup three nights a week to stay on budget.

If you have no money saved for retirement, have a whack of unused RRSP contribution room, and need the tax deduction (you're making over $40,000 a year), you'll want to put some money into your RRSP to boost your retirement savings. Remember, you should only claim as much of the deduction as you need to get a refund without lowering your taxable income too far. A good accountant will help you figure this amount out.

If you have a mortgage, you may want to pay it off. Careful now. If you're going to sacrifice your retirement savings or eliminate your emergency fund to do this, think again. For your financial foundation to be solid, all the legs of your table have to be in place or the whole thing will come toppling down.

Thinking like a CFO means balancing yesterday's obligations, which you must still fulfill (debt), with today's needs (operating expenses to run your life) and tomorrow's requirements (retirement or planned spending to replace a vehicle, for example).

If you've got all your ducks in a row and the money is truly a windfall, keep the 80/20 Rule in mind. Sock away 80% for the future and go ahead and have fun with 20%. You might want to take a longed-for vacation or establish a bequest. It is your money and you get to do whatever you want with it as long as you've dotted all your i's and crossed all your t's. Money is meant to bring you pleasure and comfort.

If you brag about being in the money because you received a lump-sum payout, don't be surprised if friends and relatives start hitting you up for loans. If you don't want money to become an issue in your relationships, do not share your financial information with friends and family. A diplomatic "John left me enough to be comfortable," or "I've got enough to see me through until I retire" will suffice if someone asks if you're financially okay.

If you decide to lend money, think like a banker. Draw up a legal document that both you and the other person sign. Include your names, the dates, a schedule for repayments, and the interest rate charged. You may want to include a third party in the room, someone unrelated or impartial, to verify you are loaning, not giving, the money. This adds a note of seriousness to the transaction. It's not just "something from Mom or Dad or Aunt Em or my brother." It's clear you are entering into a legal agreement.

I've loaned people money. I get the deal in writing and signed. Once, when the schedule of payments was not met, it was a hard phone call to make to remind the person of their obligation. The second time it happened, the phone call was easier. I suggested an automatic transfer of funds to my account and this ended the late payments.

You may decline to loan the money. CFOs say no all the time. You must never loan money you're counting on to pay bills. And if you feel the loan may not be repaid and you can't afford the loss, you must say no. You can say something like "I can see this is important to you. I wish you the best, but I am not able to help financially," or "I won't lend you money, but perhaps I can help in another way."

Don't get sucked into picking up the tab at a restaurant because people think you're rolling in money. And don't fall into the trap of being very generous with your gift giving in those early days of feeling "rich," because you'll be raising the bar. What seems like a huge amount of money today will shrink quickly. You need to make this money last as long as you do.

GROWING YOUR MONEY

Investing isn't as mysterious as it sounds. It simply means putting your money to work for you. If you stick it under your mattress and it earns you nothing, it's saved but not invested. If you stick it in a stupid account that pays you just 0.25% interest, it's invested (because you're earning interest), although you could do better.

As CFO you determine what route you will take to grow your money. Forget hot tips and what the experts say you should be doing. Investing is a highly personal experience. Only you can decide what will work for YOU.

Begin by figuring out how much risk you're willing to take. While the word "risk" may send shivers down your spine, know that all investments have some element of risk. Keeping your money in a savings account leaves you open to inflation risk, which will eat away the buying power of your money. You can tie the money up a little longer in a Guaranteed Investment Certificate (GIC) to earn more return. You can buy a bond. You can look to the stock market and choose individual shares of companies you feel have promise. Or you can decide to spread your eggs over several baskets using a mutual fund or three. Or maybe you'll just "buy the index" and go with what's happening in the markets as a whole.

The more you learn, the better prepared you will be to invest. There are investment books for beginners and lots of information online to help you learn about the choices you have for putting your money to work.

GAIL'S STORY

• •

I meet a lot of people while I'm oot and aboot and one of the questions I get most often is "What should I be investing in?" Holy moly! If you're asking me this question, you're not ready to be an investor. True investors know what they're doing; it's not just plunking down your money and hoping for the best. True investors have taken the time to learn. Some even "practise" first by building a phantom portfolio that they can track and learn from. Above all, true investors don't ask how to make their money grow; they figure it out. So after they get this lecture, the next question people usually ask is "But where do I start?" Start with indexed investing. Go online to an unbiased source and familiarize yourself with the investing world. Learn. Then do.

VICTORIA'S STORY

I used to be a stockbroker, and reading Gail's story made me laugh. Unless the person asking the question is absolutely identical to Gail in age and investing temperament and they have the same goals, time horizon, and amount of money to invest, they won't pick the same investments as Gail. And the investments will change over time. Investing is personal. And it is a lifelong process in which knowledge truly is accumulated.

WHO WILL ADVISE YOU?

With a pile of money in the bank and a lack of confidence about what to do next, your first thought may be to ask your adult children for help. You trust them and they know you, so it makes sense, right? It looks like it makes sense, but it really doesn't, since—unless your child gives investment advice for a living—they probably don't have the experience and the training to do it well. And if your child can't be completely unbiased in their recommendations, things will not work out in the long run.

GAIL'S STORY

. . . .

I've been an investor most of my life. I've reached the age and stage where I feel I have enough money. Despite saying this repeatedly, I'm often urged by advisors to get into the market so my money can keep working hard for me. But that's not where I am right now. I'm more focused on capital preservation (keeping my money) than on capital growth (making more money). It might be that advisors are much younger than I am. They have a greater risk tolerance—along with a greater need to prove something—than I do. Remember, the advisors you choose to work with have their own histories, their own agendas, and their own risk tolerance, and those may be reflected in the recommendations they make to you.

Regardless of the designation your advisor uses, the true test of their value will be how good they are at establishing and maintaining a relationship with you. Once you decide to invest, begin small, especially if this is your first step into the investment world. You're trying on the advisor's experience and expertise, and you're testing your own reactions to investing. Equity investors are prepared for the reality of fluctuating prices. If you can't handle that, you're not an equities investor. You'll have to stick to the more conservative options like bonds, mortgages, or fixed-term options like GICs, money market funds, and high-interest savings accounts.

GAIL'S STORY

. . . .

Since I'm much more conservative with my money these days, it's important that I earn as much as I can whenever I can. I shop for high-interest
savings accounts that pay better than the Big Five banks' GICs. So that
old adage of locking up your money to earn higher interest is dead as far
as I'm concerned. And I know no loyalty. If one company has a rate sale on
and is offering me a half-percent more for six months, I move my money.
It's an electronic transaction, after all, requiring only that I push some
buttons. When the premium-rate period is over, I move the money to wher-
ever I must to earn as much as I can.

There's no rule that says you can only have one advisor. If
you work with a couple of people you will, in effect, diversify
your advisory base and have a built-in check and balance for
any advice you receive. Advisors will want you to consolidate
all of your assets in one place. But you don't have to. Try two
advisors for a while and decide later if you want to consolidate.

THINKING IN FUTURE TENSE

All CFOs keep an eye on the future. They know that they may need
to delay some gratification today to cover needs down the road.

VICTORIA'S STORY

. . . .

I once gave a talk about investing. I asked the question "How many of you
waste $25 a month?" Everyone in the room put their hand up. Some people
yelled, "Multiples of $25!" I suggested they take the $25 they admitted

to wasting and, using a monthly investment program, buy into a mutual fund. Such an easy way to get into investing.

Eventually you will stop working for a living, if you haven't already. When the paycheques stop coming in, you need to replace them with income you've organized through your retirement planning.

Think of retirement income as a jigsaw: the more pieces in your puzzle, the less you need to count on only one source of income. Here are the pieces that could be part of your retirement-income puzzle:

- Canada Pension Plan (CPP)
- Old Age Security (OAS)
- Investments held in a Registered Retirement Savings Plan (RRSP) or Registered Retirement Income Fund (RRIF)
- Pension from an employer
- Income from insurance products, such as an annuity or segregated funds
- Equity in your home
- Dividend-paying stocks or interest-bearing bonds
- Rental property income
- Savings accounts
- Investments held in a Tax-Free Savings Account (TFSA)

Time is the important element in creating a retirement plan. The longer you have until you need to use the money, the more time your investment has to compound (in the case of interest) or even out its return (in the case of equity investments). The time horizon varies. As you get closer to using the money, your time horizon shortens and your investment choices must change.

If you'll need to use the money in five years or less, you're a short-term investor. Stick to fixed-income investments like bonds or high-interest savings accounts that generate a steady return while offering a higher level of capital preservation. Since you're pretty close to needing the money, you want to make sure it's there.

If you won't need to use the money for 10 years or more, you're a long-term investor. As long as you have the stomach for the risks associated, you can look to equities, which have historically outperformed all other types of investments over the long term.

VICTORIA'S STORY

I bought some segregated funds when I was 57 with part of my retirement money. I will not begin to collect a monthly income until I am 71. Locking the money away for 14 years and then receiving a benefit every month until I die was my goal when I chose this investment. I gave up access to the money in the short term in exchange for a guarantee of monthly income in the long term. That was the trade-off.

The future is not as up close and personal as yesterday or today. You know the past; it feels solid and familiar because you lived through it. The present also feels real. But the future is a bit harder to grasp because things could change. You might be single for the rest of your life or you might meet someone and pair up. You might suffer a health crisis or become the fittest you've ever been. You might lose your job or find yourself a new career. Each possibility would mean a change in plans.

GAIL'S STORY

. . . .

Alex has worked hard all his life. As a single dad, he made sure his daughter had what she needed to launch into a life of her own. And they talk about everything. "We were having dinner the other night, and I was talking about my will and what I want to happen with my stuff. Since my biggest asset is my home, I told her I won't ever marry and put her inheritance in jeopardy. I'm at the point now where I'm happy to have a relationship, but I won't put my assets at risk. Now that I have something to lose, I'm pretty much sure I'm permanently legally single."

As CFO you'll make decisions with the information you have at the moment. This information may alter as your life unfolds. But you must look forward, planning for your future even as you remain adaptable in your present. Remain agile so you're ready to integrate changes in life, health, work, or relationships. Stay open to opportunities and improvise based on new data you get.

Remember, as CEO of Everything, you're in charge of the here and now and the soon-to-come. Love yourself enough to plan for your future. It is where you will eventually live.

6 · LEARNING TO LIVE ON YOUR OWN

Recovering from the emotional earthquake that has shaken your world will take time. Even as you're coping with the daily duties of washing your face and pulling on your pants, you'll wonder how your life will ever get back to normal. You've changed, so how you interact with others will change too. You may be wiser. You're certainly more experienced. You may even be more cautious.

If you have become acutely aware of the repercussions of life now that you're counting on no one but yourself, you may have hunkered down and gone into a holding pattern. It won't last forever. You've still got some kick in your sneakers and, eventually, you'll want to have a good time. Emotional strength, like muscle strength, needs to be built up. Every time you face something and come out the other side you will feel stronger, more capable, more confident.

Your sense of belonging may have taken a huge hit. Without your mate, and the anchor of a relationship, you may be wondering where you belong. Feeling adrift is normal. (Ask any CEO and they will tell you it can be lonely at the top.)

VICTORIA'S STORY

Looking back at journals I kept after my husband died, I feel tenderness for my newly single self. This entry was made just a few months after Michael died: "'You're doing really well,' people tell me. I am putting a foot out of bed each morning on the wooden floor and rising to the occasion of the day. I begin forming the new, or nearly new, me. The dogs keep the familiar routine and I follow them. Walking down the lane, we help each other keep the patterns we know. The other—the new—patterns we're discovering as we go."

One day you'll realize you're ready to face the world again. It may come slowly or it may hit you like a bolt of lightning—you're done with being sad and lonely; you want your life back. Go get it, baby!

CRYSTALLIZE YOUR DESIRES

Companies often send executives on retreat to do the strategic planning that makes their business work over the next year, two years, five years. As CEO of Everything, you're in charge of the strategic planning. Once a desire is clear in your mind, you'll find it much easier to work to achieve it. It is self-reinforcing because your brain will consider it a task to accomplish and will get busy generating ideas on how to succeed.

Think about what the experience of becoming single (or resolved to the idea of one-is-enough) has done to change your perspective. What's different about how you see your world? What is it you want to accomplish? Crystallizing your new worldview means being able to see it in your mind. Get granular with specific details. Make it so clear you can taste it.

Nan remembers the day she stopped planning to get a new partner. "I was no longer looking to meet someone; I was looking to travel and take a cooking course. I'd just ended a relationship with a man who drank and I thought, 'I don't want to harness myself to a life of trying to keep someone else sober and jeopardize my future.' I'd worked hard to fashion a good life and realized my goal was to enjoy it, not tie myself to someone like him. I'd raised my expectations of who and what I wanted to be."

In the world of business, a mission statement condenses an organization's reason for being. It answers the questions "Who am I?" and "Why am I here?" As CEO of Everything, writing a mission statement can help you to define your intentions and your values, and clarify how you want to live your life.

Grab a pen and paper (or a whole bunch of coloured pens and loads of paper). Time to get comfortable and get quiet. Write down all the words that you believe define you, your values, and how you want to live in the world. No critiquing. No judging. Just write down the things that come to mind.

Once you've got some ideas on paper, the next step will be to tie them together in a way that helps you see how you'll live your life. Ultimately you want to come up with one paragraph (masters can boil it down to one sentence) that clearly states what's most important to you. The mission statement is a frame within which you operate. With a mission statement in place, you can then set goals to live out your mission.

VICTORIA'S STORY

Ten years ago I worked to create a map of things I felt passionate about. I described my mission statement as "Caring and thinking in new ways, and encouraging others to do the same." One of my goals was to live by a "skinny-dipping philosophy." By this I meant that wild and daring feeling I recalled from my days skinny-dipping at Skeleton Lake. Having this mindset meant I jumped at the chance to go up in a friend's small plane, hopped into the boat to go whale-watching in the Atlantic Ocean, and painted one of my rooms purple. We take actions that are aligned with our values, so getting clear about what I valued was vital.

Keep expanding your possibilities. There are many routes to achieving the things you want from life; you just have to be creative. If you love the theatre but lack funds to see performances, become an usher. You'll see productions for free. If you want to travel, house/pet-sitting might get you free accommodation. Become a cook at a camp so your kids get to go for free.

Any CEO will tell you resources are limited. It is the clever use of resources that will make the difference between whining about your dreams and making them come true. If you dig deep, you will find dozens of ways to achieve what you want from life. Thinking innovatively will move you from dreaming to doing.

Your mission statement will tell you if you are living out what you value. How many times in your typical day are you doing things that support your values? In business they call these key result areas (or KRAs). Yours might be to continually learn new things or, perhaps, to prepare for the future. Maybe you want to become socially involved. Or you might want to explore the world. If you find your focus veering away from your KRAs to the hundreds of daily duties and time-wasters that suck your energy away, you'll feel frustrated, even angry, that you're not achieving what you want.

Specific tasks are a good way to put a KRA into your daily or weekly routine. If your goal is good financial stewardship but you are in debt, what step could you take today to get closer to being debt-free? Did you rework your budget and trim excess wants? Have you spent time looking for a part-time job to get the extra money you'll need to get to debt-free forever? Are you walking your talk?

If your mission is to have a healthy lifestyle and you didn't walk around the block, eat enough fruit and vegetables, or call a pal to go to the gym, is this really what you want or what you think you should want? How can you nudge yourself to do the things that are in keeping with your mission? How can you corral your better angels to help you take action to achieve your KRAs?

Keep anything that will help remind you front and centre. Put your sneakers in the doorway before you go to bed and you're more likely to put them on and go for a walk in the morning. Keep a bowl of apples on the counter and you'll grab one to munch on when you get hungry. Make life easier for yourself by putting good choices within easy reach.

THIS CAN'T BE MY LIFE

There will be days when you feel stuck. Did you gloss over the last section while thinking, "Yeah, yeah, maybe tomorrow"?

The Law of Inertia says that a body in motion will remain in motion until some force acts upon it. The flip side is that a body at rest will stay at rest. If you feel like you're stuck, looking around wondering how the hell you got here, it will take a push to get you moving.

Have you thought, "This can't be my life," or "It sucks to be me," or "This is not what I expected"? If you thought it and did nothing about it, how do you imagine things will change? It is YOUR job, as CEO of Everything, to keep Me, Inc., operating. If you're stuck, it is you who must take action and get moving.

GAIL'S STORY

Joanie was always the quiet one, happy to tag along with the force that was her mate, Paul. She was the introvert, he the extrovert. She liked the quiet times; he brought the adventure into their lives. When Paul died, Joanie had to learn to direct her own life. With two kids and a decided preference for lying low, Joanie had to push herself out of her comfort zone so that her children wouldn't miss out because of her preference for being a house mouse.

Do something. Just one thing. If your mission statement includes the word "healthy," that means eating well. So you need to figure out what contributes to your mission and what detracts from it. Clean your refrigerator. Dump the crap. Refill your fridge with better choices. Now you've put inertia to the side and gotten movement to work for you.

VICTORIA'S STORY

Lola lost 40 pounds in one year. She began by cleaning her fridge. She realized that if she wanted to be healthier, she needed to eat healthier. So she filled her fridge with greens, carrots, chicken, tuna, and grapes. Sugar and all the other usual suspects of weight gain went into the trash. She made the first change, and it led to a second and then a third.

Don't try to do too many things at the same time. If you get so caught up in making things better that you try to do too much at once, you'll split your energy and your focus, and you'll wear yourself out. Pick one thing that you're going to do differently today and do that thing. Tomorrow (or next week) you can pick the next thing to do. Give your habits time to settle into your life. Moving slowly stops you from going off in all directions and achieving nothing.

If you've always been comfortable doing things in a certain way, it's hard to change. Have you always bought whatever you wanted whenever you wanted? It can be hard to quit cold turkey. Establishing a no-shop day is one way to start slowly. The change doesn't have to be drastic to be profound. Small steps get you to where you're going without the risk of sliding back.

GAIL'S STORY

When Tom separated he decided that since he'd always wanted to ride a motorcycle, it was time. Tom's a very social guy, so riding alone wasn't going to cut it for him. He joined a motorcycle club. Those guys ride all over the place during the good weather, sometimes spending up to eight hours on the road, eating in new places, having a blast. And when it gets too cold to ride, they get together on the regular to have dinner and shoot the breeze about riding, life, and whatever else is on their minds.

The only barrier between you and what you want to achieve is gumption. You've got to be a hard-headed hard-ass and demonstrate determination. Put inertia to the side and each step you take will create the momentum for the next step.

To keep yourself motivated and moving forward, reward yourself with a pat on the back each time you achieve a goal. Keep a list of your accomplishments and you'll increase the probability that you will stay on course. And accept that you will make mistakes. No one goes from point A to point B in a straight line. If you won't do something because you can't do it perfectly, you're going to stay stuck. We live in an imperfect world. Setting perfection as your goal only increases the likelihood of inaction or failure. Relax enough to create the life you want, even with the messes you make along the way. Give yourself permission to make mistakes, as long as you do your best.

How long have you been thinking about what you want to change in your life? How much daydreaming have you done about how life would be if only . . . ? How afraid are you that you will fail? Are you willing to be afraid and still move forward?

If you want a different life, you must take a step. No CEO stands still. Use your energy to reach your goals, rather than just dreaming, or worrying, or fighting, or crying, or moaning, or whining. A little less "thinking" and a little more "doing" is what will get you from where you are now to where you want to be.

VICTORIA'S STORY

When I first met Gail, she had just started a financial magazine for women. She asked me if I would write an article for the magazine. I did. This led to more articles, to a friendship, to writing for her blog, and now to writing this book together. Did I ever imagine this would be the happy result of writing that first article? Never. My big lesson? Get started in the direction of how you want to enjoy your life and who knows how things will turn out?

BUILDING A NEW SOCIAL NETWORK

Sometimes being alone can feel very lonely. You experience a big day at work. You see a gorgeous sunset. You read a funny story. You want to share these experiences with someone. Once upon a time you just had to turn to the person beside you to laugh, wonder at the beauty, talk out your frustration. With the other guy gone, you're going to have to find new people to share your experiences with.

Expecting your best friend to dump their family to go gallivanting with you is unrealistic. Other people have priorities, and your most successful integration with them acknowledges that reality. If your bestie values the dinner hour with their family, you may have to reconcile yourself to seeing them for lunch.

Your social life may take many forms. If you're a foodie, then a lot of socializing may happen in your kitchen or at local restaurants.

GAIL'S STORY

Ian and I love to cook new recipes together. When we're both home in Brighton, we scrounge online recipe sites to come up with interesting dishes neither one of us has eaten. We take turns going to each other's homes and experimenting with these new recipes. It's fun to share the adventure of a new dish with someone who loves to eat AND doesn't judge.

VICTORIA'S STORY

Years ago Norman said to me, "Why stress out about getting together with friends for a meal? The purpose is to see them, talk, laugh, and enjoy their company. All of this fuss about preparing days in advance and following the latest food trends is a waste. Buy a bottle of wine, a bag of veggies and dip, order a pizza, and open a tub of ice cream. Done." How true. The purpose of getting together with friends is . . . wait for it . . . getting together with friends. Food is the side dish, not the main course.

Being single doesn't mean staying home. It does mean learning how to eat out by yourself with ease. Maybe you'll take along a book or magazine to read. Perhaps you'll people-watch. Look for locations in which you can sit at a community table or eat up at the bar, where you're more likely to strike up a conversation. Know that you're among the trendsetters when it comes to eating out. According to Open Table, which is an online restaurant reservation provider, solo reservations are up 62% over the past two years.

When it comes to at-home dinner parties, invitations may

dry up or may come with an attempt at matchmaking. The only way to fix this is to be upfront about it. "I'm fine being the odd-man out," you can say. Or "I'm not really interested in being set up, so don't invite people for me. Invite people you love to have over." Eventually friends will see how comfortable you are and the awkwardness will go away.

Socializing isn't limited to the consumption of food. Go ahead, buy a concert ticket, a theatre ticket, a movie ticket. Get all dolled up and take yourself out on a date. Chat with the people around you. You are all there for the same reason, so it is easy to strike up some small talk about what you're seeing. If you want to share the experience with a friend, use your social network or your work network to find someone who wants to see the same show you do. Buy two tickets and then post on Facebook that you're looking for a companion for the evening.

Being single opens you up to experiences you would not have as a couple.

VICTORIA'S STORY

Marguerite decided to do her life differently after her mate passed away. She started striking up conversations with other single people when she travelled. "This would have never happened when I was married," she said. "I was far from home, sitting in a restaurant in New Zealand, where I met a woman who was eating alone. It turned out she was also travelling, and I got some great ideas from her."

There are all kinds of groups out there that you can join if you're looking for people with similar interests. Or you could start your own group. Someone has to go first; why not you? Love to travel? Gather people who like to share travel stories and tips. Love to read? Start a book club in your neighbourhood. Any passion is a great way to meet people with similar interests. If you try a group and it doesn't work, try another one.

VICTORIA'S STORY

Sheryl started a group. She realized small business owners like her, who had only one employee (her CEO self), could benefit from getting together with others who were in a similar situation. This is how "Chicks in Charge" came into being. Each year Sheryl gathers other CEOs for a two-day retreat in her country residence to share news, plans, laughter, and food. The group supports each member, helps to solve problems, and tests new ideas. Watching others manoeuvre through business up and downs, life's ups and downs, and meaning-of-life questions always keeps the conversation moving.

CH-CH-CHANGES

If you've recently donned the mantle of CEO of Everything, what better time to look at what's working for you socially and what you want to get rid of? Do you often say, "I must" or "I should" because you feel obligated, but deep down just don't want to anymore? If you feel you're doing things just because you've always done them, now's the time to make some changes. Do you have to send out those Christmas cards? Is it always going to be your job to host Thanksgiving dinner? Is it always your truck and your labour moving someone?

Sometimes you get on a path and can't seem to get off. Psychologists call this "path dependency." You are corralled into an activity that you keep doing because you always have. The pattern is reinforced since the feedback you get is familiar.

If you feel you've always been predictable, now could be the time to be capricious. Think your life is drab and colourless? What can you do to change that situation?

VICTORIA'S STORY

Irene and I were at an outdoor theatre venue when it began to rain. Irene laughed and said, "There was a time when I would have headed home, worried about how my hair looked. Now I just sit and wait out the rain. No one is looking at my hair, and I don't know why I ever thought they were." The nice thing about relaxing your boundaries is the feeling of calm that comes with it. You can distinguish between what is important and what you just thought was important.

You need some signals that you are no longer the person you were. Being the artist of your life means you get to paint the picture you want. Do something completely out of the ordinary for you. Try skydiving. Take a tour of the Alaskan islands. Get a new hairdo or update your wardrobe.

Grab a piece of paper and a pen and make a list of all the things you always thought you'd love to do. Is there a course you've been longing to take? A new hobby you want to try? A skill you want to acquire? Think of all the options open to you. People sometimes refer to this as a bucket list. What's on yours?

GAIL'S STORY

For most of my adult life I've dabbled with oil painting. On and off I'd grab a canvas and my heart would hum as I spread paint, texturing and mixing colours. I never kept any of my paintings. I gave a couple away when I left Toronto and threw a whole bunch more away after my marriage ended and I moved to Brighton. About a year after I retired from television production, I felt the urge to pick up brushes and knives again. With more time to focus on the painting, with no one wondering when I was coming to bed, I could spend as much time as I wanted slathering on the paint. I'm getting pretty good.

Want to put up wildly patterned curtains in your living room? Do it. Want to try being a vegetarian? Hey, what better time to try on this kind of lifestyle change? Up to now you may have felt enormously constrained, holding things together for everyone else. Now you can let loose and enjoy your freedom.

VICTORIA'S STORY

One day, Maria, a white-haired woman in her 60s, wore a red wig to work. She didn't make a fuss about it. She walked in and sat at her desk like normal. A lot of the people in the office were shocked, but Maria just proceeded as if it were a regular day. She wanted to shake things up for herself.

There are all kinds of decisions you will make that reflect where you're going with your new life. Will you keep wearing your ring? Will you change your name? How do you label yourself status-wise? Some of these things will feel small, some gargantuan. If you've worn that ring for the past 30 years, taking it off may be more of a reminder of your loss than keeping it on. If you change your name, it can be your signal to yourself and everyone else that you're done with the previous chapter of your life. If you still call yourself Mrs., instead of Miss or Ms., it may be your attempt to put up a wall to avoid unwelcome advances. As long as you are aware of why you're making your choices, you'll be fine. If you make choices unconsciously, you might find regret creeping in later.

As you set about changing, there will be people in your life who think you've lost your marbles or who express concern about how far you're drifting from the old you. If there is anything *not* worth worrying about, it is what other people think. The world will not spin off its axis because your previously coiffed hair now lives in a bun atop your head. As CEO of Everything, you will be making new choices, and you'll be responsible for what comes of those choices.

GAIL'S STORY

Kay separated after being married for 12 years. She and her ex had been in love since high school. Mario was the only man she'd ever slept with. Kay decided she was going to make up for lost time. A doll, she had no trouble getting dates. After about six months of whirlwind dating and several new sexual experiences, Kay showed no sign of slowing down. "I hope you're having protected sex," I said to her. She grinned. She was, and lots of it. Her mom, her sister, and a couple of her other friends had tried to tell her she was going overboard. When she asked me what I thought, I said, "Not my vagina, not my call."

Not every day that you're in charge of your own life will feel powerful and exciting. Being in charge of your life means some days can feel like a burden. If you start to freak out because your car heater quit, laundry is piling up, and your new boss is acting like a twat, stop. Those days, in the context of the whole, will be few, so don't let them become more important than they are. You will not be in charge of all the things that happen to you, but you're completely in charge of how you respond.

EMOTIONS, VALUES, AND DECISIONS

Just as you thought you'd got into a groove, BOOM, a wave of despair arrives. Doubt creeps in. Are you doing the right things? What if you are doing the wrong things? Rosy turns dreary. Glad turns sad. How did you get kicked out of your happy place?

This up and down happens when you're living through an emotional earthquake. According to the Holmes and Rahe Stress Scale, the death of a spouse, divorce, and marital separation are the top three things that'll wig you out and send your stress levels through the stratosphere. You're going to lose it from time to time.

Remind yourself that when you make decisions, you are using all the information you have available at the time. You are doing your best. Looking back and beating yourself up over what you should have done differently isn't fair (as long as you did your due diligence), since hindsight is always 20-20.

This sense of being the one on whose shoulders everything sits can feel impossibly heavy. You will recall how much less stress you used to feel making decisions because it didn't all come down to YOU. There was someone to bounce ideas off. Two heads were better than one. It's easy to forget that those past decisions sometimes turned out to be less successful than you'd hoped. They turned, instead, into lessons learned. And now you've got to get comfortable with the idea of making mistakes and learning more lessons. There are no guarantees even with the best information. The future is always uncertain. Your job is to ask what options are now open to you.

One way to reduce your uncertainty is to make choices that fit the life you want, not the life you had or the life other people think you should have. That means understanding your core values and making sure that the decisions you make reflect those values.

GAIL'S STORY

. . . .

My children have always come first in my life. When I was offered the opportunity to work in television, that Kids First priority was challenged. While the idea of hosting a TV show was intriguing and the money was good, I'd have to give up what was most important to me. Doing "whatever it took" to get the job would put my life out of balance and make me unhappy. In the end I did go into TV production, but it was on my terms.

Go back to your mission statement. Bring your core values to the front-and-centre position. Have you thought lately about what's most important to you, and what would take a back seat in a skirmish?

The following questions aren't meant to be the definitive test of whether your actions match your values, but they are the kinds of things you should be asking yourself before you make big decisions:

- Does this action make me happy?
- Am I being true to my mission and my values?
- Is this decision good for the environment?
- Is my next move financially wise?
- Does this action help me to meet my long-term goals?
- Will this commitment add another layer of responsibility to my already full life?
- How will this action impact my loved ones?
- Who else will this affect, how, and do I care?

If your thoughts, your feelings, and your actions are not all moving in the same direction, what are you going to do about it? You are steering the ship; where are you taking yourself?

TAKE CARE OF YOU

Being CEO of Everything can be exhausting. No doubt, you've spent a lot of time focusing and holding on tight. But too much tension will cause things to snap. Aside from being CEO and CFO, you're also the Executive Vice President of Human Resources, which means you are the person in charge of your own well-being. If you don't want to end up worn out or sick, you're going to have to take your stress management and health seriously. There's no one else around to do it!

Running on triple time will wear you out faster than a pair of cheap socks at a marathon. Make time to relax and think. Downtime gives your system a breather and lets your batteries recharge.

Think about how you like to relax. What are the things you do that leave you feeling calm and refreshed? Will you sit and read a book or hike a trail? Is taking a nap or mowing the lawn more your thing? However you choose to spend your downtime, the goal is to quiet your madly manoeuvring mind by focusing on something, anything, that you enjoy. Pick the play or the sport or the relaxation activity that releases the pressure. Build in some slack time to ease the tension. Everyone needs a pressure release; find yours and then use it (or them) to keep yourself in top form.

While everyone in your life may have ideas about what you should do, what you should say, and how you should act, no one knows you better than you do. Since you have the best view of your life—the view from inside your skin—you'll know best what's right for you. And since you'll be the one living with the consequences of your decisions no matter who had input, you had best learn to trust yourself. Family and friends may have "your best interest" at heart as they weigh in on your life, but they can't even imagine what you know about you. What seems right to them may be absolutely wrong for you. Keep reminding yourself that you've got a PhD in you. So other people's input and ideas are fine, but the decision will be yours.

GAIL'S STORY

After I left television production, people kept insisting I should go back. The shows had been such hits and people had learned so much that they couldn't imagine why I wouldn't want to continue in this very successful career. But I was done with TV. I had a very successful run, and when I could no longer make the quality TV I had fought hard to make, walking away made more sense than hating every day of my life.

Learning is part of taking care of you. When interviewed, most CEOs of major corporations stress the importance of "continuous learning." It's a buzz phrase in the biz world. Stop learning and your skills become obsolete. With life accelerating at a wicked clip, if you don't make a commitment to keeping up, you'll soon find yourself out of step with the new world around you. Research at the University of Madrid shows that reduced mental stimulation can lead to a decrease in cognitive functioning, while an enriched environment—formal or informal—helps compensate for cognitive and emotional decline. So keep challenging yourself and keep learning.

Watch the language you use to talk to yourself, since it can be very powerful. You talk to yourself more than you talk to any other person. It's hard to live with the constant criticism that comes from negative self-talk. It can be just as hard to spot when you're doing it. It sounds like this:

"Why can't you ever . . ."

"You're so stupid . . ."

"Get some control . . ."

"What the hell were you thinking?"

"Seriously, you think you can do that?"

If you heard one stranger saying similar things to another, you'd be appalled. Never mind if you overheard someone speaking as sharply to someone you love—you'd be furious.

Some people's self-talk sounds cruel because they genuinely believe they're giving themselves tough love. If you think it's self-indulgent to be compassionate with yourself, that's a nasty tape you're running. Get rid of it. You don't need that inner critic to keep you motivated. And, no, you're not being selfish if you're looking out for yourself and making sure you are cared for. In fact, the only way you can really feel compassion for others is by feeling compassion for yourself.

The things you don't feel you do well aren't failures; they're your opportunity to learn and grow or, failing that, to give the task to someone else. Focusing on what you do wrong doesn't teach you how to do it better. Instead, focus on what you do right and on what you'll do differently next time. Learn to speak in terms of the progress you've made:

"I am going forward."

"I'm feeling better this week."

"I am improving."

"My intention is to keep moving."

If you've been tough-talking for a long time, being gentle with yourself won't come naturally. It is so easy to focus on the negative. But showing loving kindness to yourself, the person who is slogging through this change, is worth the work. And you deserve it. Remember, as CEO of Everything, you are your biggest asset. Value the asset that is you.

SETBACKS

As you begin to live again, you will encounter setbacks that make you feel like the progress you've made is slipping away. One day you were happily CEO of Everything and then BAM, there you are, back at square one.

VICTORIA'S STORY

While I was working on this book, my beloved dog Pongo died. He was a 15½-year-old golden retriever. When my husband died, our two dogs provided comfort and kept me in a routine. When Stukie died, I still had Pongo and our routine. Without the last member of my pack, I felt lost. All the triggers for my day seemed to have gone. Morning, up and dressed, and walk the dog. Cancel. Make breakfast for Pongo and give him medication. Cancel. There were dozens of ways we routinely orbited each other. Now I needed to unlearn all those patterns and learn new ones.

As you move along your new path there will be twists and turns. Setbacks can be about identity. A loss of a job may affect your confidence. Setbacks can be about chaos in your well-planned life. The stress of illness, of caring for an aging parent, of dealing with a disabled child can make you feel like you should just duck and hide. When it feels easier to lie down than it is to push forward, push forward anyway. The key is to keep moving.

Embrace routines. While you're doing the dailies of life, try to stay in the moment and be where you are. If you're cutting carrots, focus on cutting carrots. Letting your mind wander to the confusion that's curdling your composure won't help. Staying in the present and fully experiencing whatever it is you're doing will.

Find your joy. It may be in small things: the laughter of your children, a quiet cup of tea on the porch as you watch the birds, a sitcom that always makes you laugh. Look for happy moments and celebrate them, so you don't forget that more happy moments are around the corner.

GAIL'S STORY

. . . .

My daughter, Alex, has been watching the sitcom *Friends* for over a dozen years. She practically knows the 10 seasons by heart. When things go wrong in her day—when she gets frazzled, if she's feeling a little blue—she joins her Friends, laughs along with them, watches them deal with their struggles. It calms her down. She's already worn her way through two sets of discs.

Give yourself permission. Whether you want to express your anger, fear, or sadness, give yourself space to do so as you work through your challenges. It helps to have a friend or two with whom you can vent. These need to be people who are willing to listen without a) taking on your pain or b) judging you and whatever has happened to you. "Single" doesn't mean toughing things out solo. Reach out. A friend who is willing to "just listen" is worth their weight in gold.

Do you like to journal? Write it out. Do you love to sing? Sing it out.

GAIL'S STORY
. . . .

When my second marriage ended after nine years, I would turn on Gloria Gaynor's "I Will Survive" and belt it out at the top of my lungs. Over and over. I needed to remind myself that I was stronger than I was feeling.

Couples have setbacks. Families have setbacks. And so will you. Dealing with a setback and moving on is the mark of a truly empowered CEO.

COPING WITH TURBULENCE
So what can you do when you encounter the obstacles that all CEOs inevitably face?
1. You can rise above it.
2. You can drop below it.
3. You can flank it.
4. You can fly through it.

Rising Above. When you rise above turbulence, you decide that getting involved brings nothing positive into your life and you choose to fly above the fray. Think big picture and keep your eye on what is really important. People are fighting over the will: You decide that it is not your job to fix this problem. Let them sort it out as long as it doesn't affect you. Colleagues at work are unhappy with the new office hours: You ask yourself if this is a big deal. If not, look skywards. Not every problem is yours to solve. Get up in the clouds and enjoy the view.

Dropping Below. When you drop below, you keep your head down for a while and give the situation some time to resolve itself. Many issues are based on clashing values. Gerry values green space and Alex likes the convenience of having a shopping centre close by. They're bumping up against each other regarding town planning and development. Do you really want to join the fight? If this isn't something you want to spend time on (or have time to spend on), fly under the radar for a while. That may mean passing on coffee dates or neighbourhood gatherings where this issue comes up. But that's better for you than listening to one more battle being fought.

Flanking. If you flank something, you manoeuvre to the side to skirt the turbulence. You're exercising your creative muscles and choosing a different route. You bring a salad to a party you know consists of wings and beer so you can join the fun and still stay on your eating plan. When someone suggests a gift exchange and you are already at the end of your budget, you propose everyone bring something they made themselves because homemade gifts are the best kind. Flanking means taking a different tack to achieve the goal.

Flying Through. Flying through may mean you're in for a fight. There are storm clouds up ahead, you see them clearly, and you plan to meet them head-on. If you are getting divorced, you need to obtain some of the pension income of your former spouse. Forget about being compliant; you need to become a tiger and fight for your rights. If you've always avoided conflict, you may have to learn to be fierce. When your sister asks you for yet another loan but hasn't repaid the last one, this is the moment you say no. You might be shunned or insulted, but CEOs don't avoid tough decisions. The buck stops with you.

Will there be pushback as you begin to implement your preferences? There could be. Will people resist your actions, push harder, or call you selfish and self-centred? Maybe. Will folks ridicule or dismiss your wishes? Perhaps. Will you give in or give up? ABSOLUTELY NOT. If the situation has been set up as a "one person wins and one person loses" event, do you want to be the loser in your life?

VICTORIA'S STORY

When I told a couple of spendthrifts I did not have money to loan them, the wife stopped speaking to me and no longer sent me Christmas or birthday cards. When I asked the husband about it, saying I felt punished, he sided with her and said, "Well, you'll just have to get over it." That was exactly what I needed to hear. I got over it.

Developing a backbone and sticking to your guns may not come easily if you haven't done it before. You may do it clumsily the first time. But you'll be better the second time. And eventually, being in the pilot's seat will feel perfectly natural.

Don't be afraid of conflict. Conflict can be a good thing. But it should not be your first choice for how you handle turbulence. Before it gets to the point of choosing weapons, try diplomacy. You can always escalate to fighting, but if you go straight to battle, the final outcome is either surrender or annihilation.

WHAT TO DO NEXT

Now that you are CEO of Everything, the ever-expanding list of duties that fall on your shoulders needs to be assessed, reordered, and pared down.

The word *analysis* comes from the Greek and means to loosen or undo. When you analyze, you take apart the idea and reconsider its value. Since nobody can do it all, you need to be conscious of when you are reaching your limits. And that means taking the time to do some analysis so you're sure you are expending energy where you want to. You may be able to double-time it through your life for a short while, but you won't be able sustain it. As CEO, you must think of the long game. This means knowing your limits and saying, "I'm done," "That's it for me," or "Enough."

New issues will keep cropping up, and you must deal with them. You are in charge of it all. So you'll have to decide what's urgent, what's important, and what you can ignore.

VICTORIA'S STORY

Moving into my current house, I knew the electric furnace was 18 years old. When the first January bill arrived at nearly $500, I thought, "I'm not going to make it with these costs." I shut off the energy-sucking furnace and used my wood stove for two years. My backup plan, the wood stove, became my primary source of heating. Costs went down and so did my body temperature. I bought an infrared heater for the kitchen and another for downstairs. I put on layers of clothing and kept slippers at the door for visitors. I coped. Then came the day I fractured my wrist. Wrist wrapped in a cast, I knew my pioneering ways of chucking wood were over and I had to put in a new furnace.

Most of us have a dozen or 20 things we need to get done, and only enough time to do six. The once-shared to-do list is now all yours. So how do you decide what must get done now and what can wait? Sometimes it depends on the level of panic in someone else's voice.

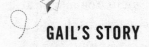

GAIL'S STORY

Sometimes things crop up and, despite my careful planning, everything else gets shunted aside. Like the morning Alex was late for rehearsal and needed something for lunch (she'd be there for six hours with no break). I heard the panic in her voice, dropped what I was doing, and made her life easier. When I was done fixing what was broken, I was late! Clearly I wasn't going to get it all done.

It helps to know what your must-dos are for each day. If you use a list (please say you're using a list, since it's the best way to get crap out of your head) and you're having one of those days, grab a highlighter and run it over the three things that just have to get done if your world is to continue spinning smoothly. Once you've got those three things done, you'll have room to manoeuvre because the biggies are out of the way.

Cut the distractions. Turn off the radio, the TV, your email, your cellphone . . . whatever it is that keeps grabbing your attention away from the urgent thing that must be done. Be honest about what you don't want to do. You're way better off just saying so—damn what people think—and living a real life than creating a bottleneck in your life so you have a good excuse for not helping your mother with her grocery shopping.

Make an appointment with yourself at least once a week to review your to-do list and prioritize, creating space in your life for yourself. If you think it's so much easier just being reactive, the truth is it can be emotionally exhausting. By being reactive you're allowing yourself to be tossed from hither to yon by whatever calamitous breeze is blowing by. If you want to be in control, make time—even if it's just 20 minutes—and be by yourself so you can plan your next week. Update your to-do list, prioritize what should happen so the world doesn't end, and build in some "Me Time" while you're at it.

7 · DEALING WITH THE STUFF

Somewhere in your very old reptilian brain lives a fear: the fear that no matter how much you have it won't be enough. Not enough canned tuna, books, bottles of hand cream, shoes, towels, baseball caps, drinking glasses, or pens. It's why you find it easy to overbuy but so, so hard to get rid of things you no longer need. Whatever you already have just never seems to be enough.

It is easy to see where these messages of "buy more" come from. Look at any magazine and you will be bathed in messages of how much more attractive you would be with this clothing, cologne, or car.

There were times in your life when you had less and you did very well.

GAIL'S STORY

When I was in my 20s, making about $16,000 a year, I remember thinking to myself that if I were ever able to make $30,000, I couldn't possibly spend it all. That would be so much money! And yet, $30K, $40K, $50K got spent. I went from shopping the sales at Fairweather to buying full price in some much more chi-chi stores. That's the thing about stuff—there's always something newer, something brighter, something cooler you can spend money on. It took me a while to get off the hamster wheel, but when I did, it was incredibly liberating not to be bossed around by a constant desire to acquire.

When Bag Lady or Homeless Guy Syndrome threatens to take over, you can't let those rampant thoughts scare you into doing dumb things. You've got to move out of your old, reptilian brain, into your newer, more intelligent frontal cortex and behave like the rational human being you are. Otherwise you'll find yourself a slave to your old brain, doing things that make no sense.

VICTORIA'S STORY

Emily travelled a fair amount for business and brought home all the sample-size toiletries from hotels. At one point, she filled a dresser so full the top drawers ended up collapsing on the bottom ones and then they all fell on the floor. Em just couldn't let go. "I may need them when I am old and poor," she reasoned. She continues to gather them to this day.

As CEO of Everything, you are head curator of your possessions. Just as a museum cannot show every artefact and an art gallery cannot display every painting and sculpture, you must decide what will stay and what needs to go to a new home.

GAIL'S STORY

My good friend Lily is a minimalist. Every time I go to visit there's less and less stuff. A single mom at 18, she used to have way more crap in her apartment. "After Paul left home, I found myself paring back," she told me as she handed me a spoon to stir the pasta sauce. "My mother had a square egg maker. Why would anyone need a square egg maker?" Visitors to Lily's place sometimes ask if she's moving because the space has been so "decluttered." "There are things I want to be able to see that are special," she told me. "I don't want them hidden by a bunch of crap."

WOULD YOU PAY TO MOVE IT?

Whether you have recently become widowed or gotten divorced, there comes a time when you have to deal with all the stuff you've surrounded yourself with. If you're leaving, what will you pack and take with you? If your mate has died, what will you do with his or her stuff? If you find you must downsize, what will you no longer have space for?

A great question to ask yourself when you're weighing whether or not to keep something is "Would I pay to move it?"

GAIL'S STORY

When I left my last marriage, I had to pack for myself and my two children even as I worked a full-time job, which included being on the road two days of the week. It was exhausting. I was brutal in my culling. I packed boxes and boxes of books—I love my books—but left as many behind as I took. I packed exactly the things I would need for my kitchen and no more. Ditto the furniture.

I only took two things that have subsequently become redundant: a curio cabinet and a piano. I'm not sure why I took the curio cabinet, except that it had come with me from my previous marriage. And as for the piano, the kids have left home and there's no one to play it anymore. Anyone want a piano?

It's time to take an inventory of what you own. Go from room to room in your home and count up what you have. How many DVDs? How many towels? How many screwdrivers? As you look at each pair of shoes, each piece of furniture, each tchotchke, ask yourself if you would pay good money to move it. The next question to ask yourself is this: "If I don't value this enough to pay for it to be moved, why am I keeping it?"

Unless you plan to die in the home you now live in, in which case all your crap will be someone else's problem, you're going to have to move it one day. If you don't want to be overwhelmed by the massive amount of stuff you've accumulated, it's time to decide what's really important to you and what it's time to cull.

VICTORIA'S STORY

Two years after Michael died, I decided to move. Most of my stuff sat in storage while I lived in a friend's guest house and looked for a new home. When I was finally reunited with my worldly possessions, I kept asking myself, "Where did all this stuff come from?" I would unwrap something, look at it, then rewrap it and put it back into the moving box. I drove carloads of boxes to the thrift store. Money down the drain to both purchase and then pay for storage. Determining what I valued before the move would have made better sense. I'm not going to make that mistake again!

We surround ourselves with so much stuff. We spend hours acquiring or planning what to acquire next. In the end much of it is little more than clutter. It is remarkably uplifting to decide what we really value and lose the clutter.

Want to see how it feels? Grab a shopping bag and walk around your house; you're looking for five things to put in that bag. These are five things you're not that fond of, five things that don't add anything significant to your life. Maybe five things you've outgrown or haven't used in the last year. Each thing you choose to put in the bag will bring you one step closer to a sigh of relief. If you have a material streak—but I might need it!—then this lesson is even more important. You are not your stuff. But your stuff can get in the way of who you really are.

We don't mean this to be an intellectual exercise. We want you to do this. Put down the book, grab a bag, and go find five things. We'll wait.

Got them? Was it hard, or did you find it very easy to put five things in the bag? Would you have been able to do 10? 20? Isn't it amazing just how much stuff we manage to surround ourselves with? Now take that bag of five things to the thrift store if they will be useful to someone else. If no one else would want them either, recycle or dump them.

The things you surround yourself with should hold real value for you, not simply be a pile of stuff. Ask yourself:

- When was the last time I used this (like your sewing machine or your guitar or your skates)?
- Where is this going to go in my new place or newly

redefined space? If you're leaving it in a box just in case, get rid of it.

- How valuable is it really? (We value stuff emotionally, but the financial value isn't always there, which is why you don't include personal effects on your net worth statement.)

VICTORIA'S STORY

After the lessons learned in my last move, now I imagine that everything I bring in to the house I must carry on my back when I move. I ask myself, "Would I be willing to physically carry it?" This keeps me from accumulating more. I've sold lawn furniture, chandeliers, jewellery, a fan, bookcases . . . it's a long list.

Only you can determine your criteria for keeping that chair, comforter, or circular saw. But you must have criteria. Maybe it must be practical. Or absolutely fabulous. Or something that makes you smile when you look at it.

If you are a "sentimental value" kind of person, if you say things like "My kids gave me this," or "This used to be my mother's," it's even more important that you use the criteria you've determined to eliminate the weight of your past decisions. Get a box, no bigger than a large hat box, and put your sentimental stuff in that box. You can only keep as much as will fit in that box. The rest has to go!

You can come up with all kinds of excuses for keeping things. Recognizing that it is fear making you hold on to all that stuff is the first step. It doesn't matter that whatever IT is was "expensive." And no, you're not going to fix it "someday." Nor does it count if you used to use it all the time. The fact that you haven't touched it in the last two years says enough about its value in *this* space and time. That's all you need to keep in mind when deciding if it stays or if it goes.

LETTING GO CAN BE EMOTIONAL

Moving forward is about releasing what no longer fits your life so you can make room for what will come next. But letting go can be very emotional. You are looking at the accumulation of things that represent your past. Opening a wedding album to scan the photos will bring back memories. Taking out your child's refrigerator art will bring smiles or tears or both. What will happen if you don't keep these memory markers? Are you afraid you'll lose your history? Are you afraid you'll lose someone else's?

Many of our most beloved items are memory joggers. We hold fast to them so we can keep a memory alive. Do you have hundreds of printed photos of your first child? Have you kept every piece of memorabilia you collected on your European vacation? Do dead flowers and ticket stubs fill up corners of your drawers? These markers for events in your life may seem precious, but as you're building your new life you will want to make room for new memories.

GAIL'S STORY

I have moved 29 times in my life. Three of the moves happened while I was still a child. All the rest have been under my own steam. The biggest move, the one from Jamaica to Canada, meant I had to leave a lot behind. I made a memory box out of a cardboard box and stuck the things inside that I wanted to keep to remind me of my early life. I learned an important lesson having to consolidate for that big move: it doesn't take a lot to bring a memory back, and most of what I need I can fit into a single box.

If you come to the end of the summer and realize you did not use your canoe or your pool noodles, your tent or your bicycle, isn't it time to offer them to someone who will get some use and pleasure from them? If your sewing machine is doing nothing more than gathering dust, isn't it better that someone who loves to sew has it? Instead of holding on "just in case," be generous and pass along the things that are no longer doing their jobs for you. Nothing was made to sit in a garage or closet. Let someone else put those things to work.

Letting go can be sad. Maybe you've decided to sell your mate's car because they will never drive it again. Or you've decided to get rid of the mug your ex used to have morning coffee in from back when you still shared a life. Dealing with losses means grieving, but holding on to stuff doesn't make the grieving any easier, so let go.

Begin by giving yourself permission. Acknowledge that while you may want to hold on to every trinket, it is stifling to keep your memories stored in things that do little more than take up space. If you aren't displaying it, using it, or enjoying it, or if it has ceased to serve its purpose, then it's time for it to go. Say goodbye to the baby clothes, the crockpot, that knick-knack from your honeymoon. (With digital photography, you don't have to drown in the physical stuff. Go ahead and take as many pictures as you like and then look at the digital album as you breathe in all the space you created.)

HELP! I DON'T KNOW WHERE TO START

You do it one step at a time and one room at a time. Let's use your bedroom as an example, since that's where you start and end your day.

Step One. Take everything out of your bedroom except the bed and heavy furniture. Empty the closet, bookshelf, night table. Put all the stuff you move out of your bedroom in the hall, the living room, dining room. The only rule is that *this stuff must be in the way of managing your daily life.* If you move it to the basement or a spare room, you can just close the door and avoid dealing with it, so you must put it annoyingly within your sight. Congratulations, you just overcame your inertia.

Step Two. Go back to your empty bedroom and wonder aloud about how you want to live in it. Do you want a cozy feeling, tidy feeling, comfortable feeling, secluded feeling, frisky feeling? Is it a sanctuary, an escape, a spa, a nest, a pleasure palace? You get to decide.

Step Three. Rearrange the furniture to achieve the mood you want. What's missing? Make a list of the things you may need to create the room of your dreams.

GAIL'S STORY

. . . .

I love my bedroom. It's my favourite room in my little house. And each time I walk into it I think, "It's so pretty." After sharing manly bedrooms—heavy wooden furniture, dark colours—with husbands for years, I finally got the room that makes me happy. The walls are periwinkle. The furniture is white wicker and there are, perhaps, a dozen plants. I have two—count 'em, TWO—feather beds on top of my mattress. And every time I change my sheets (always white sheets), I sprinkle lavender oil onto them so when I get into bed the comfort envelops me.

Step Four. Time to clean the windows, wash the window coverings, vacuum the floor. You might decide to repaint in a colour that is more in keeping with your new vision for your bedroom. You are reassembling your new room—your new life—physically and mentally.

Step Five. Now it's time to put your clothes back into your closets and drawers. But first, decide what you really want to keep and what should go. How many pairs of pants do you love to wear or need to keep? Count everything and decide on the optimal number. Didn't realize you owned 16 fleece tops? Time to pick your 10 favourites.

VICTORIA'S STORY

. . . .

When I sorted my closet I discovered I owned 33 pairs of pants. Winter, summer, dress, and sports pants as well as jeans. Too many for a woman who works from home. I decided that 12 pairs would be ample, so I've started culling. I'm not down to my goal just yet; it's a work in progress.

As you're doing this, you may find holes in your wardrobe that you need to fill, so jot down some notes. You're not rushing out to buy a whole new wardrobe; you're making a list that you can fill over time.

What other pieces will you put back into your bedroom to create the feeling you want? Love to read in bed? Put a selection of books on your bedside table. Enjoy the flicker of candlelight as you do your evening journalling? Find a candle, put it in a pretty dish, and add it to your dressing table. What pictures will you hang on the wall? How many pillows will you put on your bed? As the room begins to take shape, keep asking, "Is this the room I want to start and end my day in?"

Everything else you took out of your room—the remains now sitting in the hall, the living room, the dining room— needs to be bagged for donation, sold, or given to someone else. It no longer belongs in your beautiful new bedroom.

You may not be able to turn your bedroom into your perfect room in a single day, so be patient. It may take a weekend to accomplish it all. Or you may choose to let your nest evolve over time as you find each perfect piece to complete the picture you've painted for yourself. Give yourself time to make your new space yours, anticipating the outcome as you close your eyes. When you finally get it just the way you want it, you'll have enjoyed the journey.

I had a wall in my bedroom that called for a piece of furniture. At first I thought it was going to be another piece of wicker. But each time I saw something I thought might work, it just wasn't IT. It took me six years to find the piece that was the perfect fit. I parked in front of a small store that had a sofa table sitting out front with items on display. It was exactly the size and feel I wanted to complete that space in my room.

Giving away the clothing (and other stuff) of a loved one who has died can be a tricky business. Part of the difficulty comes from the confirmation that there is no longer a body to wear the familiar garments (or use the stuff). They hold the smell of your lost one and you don't want to lose that scent. You remember the feel of that shirt on your face. You don't want to look at empty drawers and empty cupboards because they affirm your loss over and over.

This isn't something you have to rush. The right time will come and you will know it. Or someone who loves you will help. When you are ready, offer friends and family the option of choosing a memento each. Encourage people who loved your mate to claim what they would like because you will not be keeping it. It's time for you to move on.

Keep a few reminders. Opening your closet and seeing a familiar bathrobe or shirt can be comforting. But hanging on to the golf clubs, the full set of workshop tools, or your loved one's entire collection of music isn't healthy.

Carly didn't change the sheets on the bed for weeks after her mate died. She said, "I still smell his scent on them." Frank's wife wore a specific cologne, so he kept the bottle, opening it when he needed to feel connected to her. Our sense of smell is the most powerful trigger of memories.

Whatever rituals you perform to get you through the divestiture of the stuff is fine. You're in charge of the final scene of this show, and you'll know what to do and when. If others think you're a little weird, so be it. Their discomfort is not your concern. Go at your own pace, and keep a few of the things that will bring you happy memories.

ADJUST YOUR ACQUISITION BEHAVIOUR

As CEO of Everything, you are responsible for inventory management. Once you've reduced the clutter, your goal is not to let new acquisitions start creeping back in. Think of it as keeping space in your home so you can breathe. That means having just the right amount of things for you.

If you find yourself living alone for the first time in ages, early days will find you buying for more than one person. We've been conditioned to "buy big and save." But family sizes of most things are too big for your single needs. While it costs more per unit to buy smaller sizes, it actually costs less when you consider how much you stop throwing away. Time to establish some new shopping criteria.

GAIL'S STORY

. . . .

When my children left home it took a while to adjust to cooking for one. I often ended up eating the same thing to get rid of all I'd bought. Then I smartened up. I could eat more of the things I loved because I didn't have to spend anywhere near as much keeping the fridge full for my monster eaters. I decided to keep the food I used to store in my freezer and cupboards at the supermarket. I bought only enough to last me a few days and then I went back to the market and stocked up again. I filled my freezer only when things went on special, like my favourite mushroom pizza at 60% off, or prime roasts at half price. I used the rest of the space to store my big-cook-up meals: lasagna, mac and cheese, soups, stews, anything I made a lot of at once and could then use when I just didn't feel like cooking. I don't throw much away anymore.

Food can be presented so enticingly at the store. You walk down the aisles of the grocery store thinking, "That looks interesting," and you find yourself at home with deep-fried onions, eggplant, six cans of beans that were on sale, a jar of roasted artichokes, and cranberry marmalade, none of which you intended to buy. Store merchandisers are world-class tempters.

If you aren't meal planning and shopping with a list, you're at the whim of all those smart marketing schemes designed to make you spend more money. Keep a grocery list on your fridge. As you run out of stuff or identify what you'll be cooking next, add what you need to your list. And when you go shopping, buy NOTHING that isn't on your list. (If you want to have a small amount of money set aside for taking advantage of great in-store specials, add a little extra to your grocery budget so you can stock up when prices are fabulous.)

In Canada, families drop about $6,000 a year at the store for food. Singles spend about half that. What you spend will depend on your budget, your dietary requirements, and your taste buds. There's no right or wrong amount—only what works for you. And as long as you're not wasting food or spending more than you've planned, you're fine.

Be conscious when you're shopping so you don't fall into old habits like chucking things into the cart on a whim. Shopping with a list helps to eliminate the struggle between the emotional and rational parts of your brain. Don't buy more than you need. Just because it's on sale doesn't make it a good deal unless you actually end up using it all. And if you only have a few things on your list, skip the big grocery cart. You'll be less tempted to pick up impulse items if you have to carry them in your arms or a hand-basket.

A freezer can be a frenemy. It holds those pre-made chilis, soups, and stews you whipped up so you don't have to cook from scratch every night. But it also gives you a place to hide your shopping mania. Resist the urge to pack that sucker to the hilt.

GAIL'S STORY

. . . .

I've developed a routine that keeps me from turning my freezer into a black hole. Twice a year I empty my freezer completely. I'm not going to take credit for being disciplined. Fact is, my freezer doesn't self-defrost. The first time I had to defrost it manually, I swore up a blue streak. But then I found the three packs of ground beef I'd bought on sale stuck way at the back. And was that chicken? It was barely recognizable with all the freezer burn. So my non-self-defrosting freezer became my friend. Now when I'm approaching defrost day, I start using up all the stuff in my freezer. Way less waste. And when I pack whatever I've stored in my cooler during the defrost process back into the freezer, I stick an "eat me first" label on it.

INVENTORY YOUR STUFF

If you've decided that you have too much stuff and want to simplify, the first step is to take inventory of what you have so you can a) see just how bountiful your life is, b) decide how much is enough, and c) choose the things that are most important to you. Then you can get rid of the rest.

One way to inventory your stuff is by category. How many dishes do you have? When was the last time you used the blue, cut-glass wedding gift? How much of your enormous book collection do you plan to reread or refer to? Library book sales are always looking for donations. How many of those magazines you subscribe to every year remain unread? Time to cancel some subscriptions. How much time do you spend dusting your knickknacks? Keep the things that give you pleasure when your eye lights upon them. Lose the things that make you cringe each time you think of dusting them. If you haven't rollerbladed since the 1990s or ice-skated since Obama was elected president, it's time to pass that stuff on to someone who will get joy from using it. Kids' toys, bed linens and towels, crafts, and hobbies paraphernalia all have a tendency to accumulate. Weed out what you're using from what's just taking up space. Donate anything still in its original packaging or bearing a price tag.

When my children were small, just prior to Christmas and birthdays I would scour their toy inventory for what they weren't using and either donate it or hide it, so I could wrap and re-gift it to them on a day to be chosen later. Sometimes too much choice can be as bad as not enough. By limiting their choices (and making room for what was coming) I kept the piles under control.

Your objective in taking inventory is to eliminate the surplus. Do you really need dozens of knives in the drawer? How many drills are enough drills? When was the last time you reached for that platter, tray, or serving dish? Sell whatever you can on Craigslist, Kijiji, or at a yard sale so you have the cash to do something you really want to.

DO YOU NEED A CAR?

People with cars drive on average only one and a half hours per day, according to Zipcar. Are you spending a small fortune on a vehicle that sits idle for 22 and a half hours a day?

Corrine grew up with a single mother who worked hard to give her a good life. A lot of the choices her mother made are still reflected in Corrine's life. "I've never needed a car," she told me. "I grew up without one, so it's of very little interest. I knew a car would put me over the edge financially. I had a pretty big budget for taxis, about $200 a month. That and transit got me around comfortably with no accountability for a car, insurance, parking, or maintenance."

For some people a car is a necessity. But for many more, a car is something to be acquired, paid for, and maintained, with not a lot of benefit. If you have the option of taking public transit or of renting a vehicle only when you need it, think about why you're keeping your car. Walking to your destination or riding your bicycle will not only save you heaps of money, it'll mean you can have an extra slice of pie after dinner.

Driver's licence fee, licence plates, insurance, gas, maintenance, parking, fuzzy dingle balls to hang from the rear-view mirror, car washes—it all adds up. The Canadian Automobile Association (CAA) says that it costs $6,424 a year to keep a car on the road. Statistics Canada says it costs another $2,232 to put fuel in it. Can't you think of anything else you'd rather do with that $8,656? And that doesn't take into account what you're paying in monthly loan or lease costs.

Time to think about whether the convenience of a car is worth the price. Having added up all the costs and weighed them against the convenience, you might decide to ditch your car.

VICTORIA'S STORY

When Marc and Lesley moved from a house into a two-bedroom downtown condo, they rid themselves of oodles of stuff. They also found they could walk most places or take public transit. Since they spend lots of time travelling, they decided to sell their car rather than pay to have it sit in the parking garage for so much of the year.

In our consumption-driven world, it's easy to find ourselves always wanting just a little bit more. But one of the biggest lessons a body can learn is to define "enough" for themselves. How will you know when you have enough? Enough food in your cupboards. Enough clothes in your closet. Enough nail polish, screwdrivers, yarn, underwear, mugs.

Striving is a part of the human existence. Without striving, we'd still be hunting and gathering. There's nothing wrong with ambition or wanting. But always wanting more, never being content with what we have, that can be exhausting.

GAIL'S STORY
. . . .
When I retired from TV I decided I had enough clothes. I'm not a big shopper anyway, but there's a little store in Brighton, Dragonfly, that I love. And I can always manage to find something I'd like to buy. Thing is, I've got enough clothes. So I made a deal with myself: I decided not to buy anything new until I'd worn through one-third of my wardrobe. And then it would be one in, one out.

At some point you have to take stock of your bounty and stop saying "a little more." Instead you have to focus on the "enough" that you have in your life. Knowing you have enough—of anything—is a gift. You have to keep that sense of enough front and centre in your mind for when the Gimmies come to get you. They will. You'll be watching some decor-porn on television, flipping through some fancy-schmancy magazine, listening to someone talk about their new whatever, and the Gimmies will whisper into your brain, "Oooo, you want that, don't you? You really want that." You can choose to say right back, "No, thanks, I have enough."

8 · WILL YOU STAY OR WILL YOU GO?

There are two kinds of people in the world: those who are rooted and live in the same area for their entire lives, and those who wander, living in different places. For the first, the familiar is so important they'll move heaven and earth to stay put. For the second, divorce or widowhood or deciding to go it alone is a great reason to pack up and experience the view from another location.

GAIL'S STORY

Portia decided that her high-paying executive position was working against her values, so she quit. "When I decided to leave the big job it was MY decision. If I'd had a partner I might not have had the freedom to make the tough call." Then Portia packed up her life and moved halfway across the country. "I wanted to be closer to my family. I'm the oldest of three and I've played the role of financial safety net for my siblings. I've always known that I have to financially support myself and be able to help out when needed. To me, it's part of being knitted together as a family. The move made sense financially and geographically."

Whether you stay where you are or move to a new place might be dictated by your financial circumstances or familial need, or it may be a case of too much house for li'l ol' you. Or you may make a decision because you dread the idea of being lonely. While personal preference plays a part, it's not the only deciding factor. As CEO of Everything, sometimes it'll be up to you to make the choice.

VICTORIA'S STORY
· ·

My mother is in her 80s and lives in a house overlooking a river where boats enter one of the Great Lakes. She was born on the Isle of Man and water is important to her. She spends a lot of time on her own. Whenever I call, she's on her iPad doing Pinterest or watching PBS historical or nature programs on TV. In the winter she goes to a place in Florida with access to the water. She swims in the pool and gets to see her friends daily. The winter half of her time is social, the summer half of her time less so. She's created two lives that suit her, and she enjoys both thoroughly.

If you are a wanderer and you've moved locations multiple times, you're no stranger to change. You may revel in starting fresh. Packing and unpacking, establishing new routines, and uncovering new routes are all part of the challenge and excitement of a new place. But even as you embrace the new, the fresh, the yet unseen, there will also be some stress. Changing geography does not mean your problems vanish. Wanderers just have a greater skill set for starting again.

I LOVE WHERE I LIVE

Staying may be just the right choice for you to make. As long as you can afford to maintain the place and it meets your needs, stay put.

If you are rooted, you like the familiarity of knowing where the grocery store is, when the gym opens, and not having to order at the diner because they already know what you like. It seems that for your whole life you've greeted people with a wave and stopped to catch up on news at the gas station or local coffee shop. You can get around with your eyes closed.

Changing your status in a community where everyone knows everyone else can make you the talk of the town. And while you may like the familiar, staying put means you may run into your former mate, or your ex-in-laws, or the people who chose a side and it wasn't yours! You'll have to steel yourself for those run-ins.

Staying put means you don't have to disrupt the children's lives: they can keep going to the same school, keep hanging with the same friends. And if you have a support system, that can be what saves your sanity as you move through this transition.

If you lack the stomach for dismantling your connections, staying put will work as long as you have the financial resources to do so without wearing yourself paper-thin. That means your shelter costs should not create a strain on your budget.

Judging by the letters I get, people seem to be under the impression that owning your home outright means you've got your shelter costs on lockdown. I like to point out that I live in a paid-for home, and the carrying costs on my house—property taxes, insurance, maintenance, and utilities—ran to just under $1,400 a month in 2015.

You will also have to consider the real estate market in the decision-making equation. If markets are up substantially, selling and finding a smaller place will put a whack of cash at your disposal for other things. But if the markets are fragile, holding on to your home may make more sense than taking a loss, especially if the home was a significant part of your settlement or you used a large part of your insurance benefits to pay off your mortgage.

Staying put means wearing your thick-skin jacket for at least a little while. If you've determined you will embrace your singleness wholeheartedly, you may still have to endure the multiple times people say things like "You just haven't met the right person," or "How is dating life going?" or "Are you still a swinging single?" Some days you may wonder if there is nothing else to talk about but the state of your personal life and how on track you are to meet someone in order to become unsingle.

CAN I AFFORD TO STAY?

Part of a CEO's job is to look at the company's books to make sure costs are in line with the income being generated. You need to look at your budget to make sure your shelter costs work for you, not against you.

If you are renting, what percentage of your income are you spending on your digs? The rule of thumb is to spend no more than 35% of your net income on keeping a roof over your head. If you have no consumer debt—things like credit card, line of credit, or overdraft balances—sucking on your cash flow, you can afford to spend up to 50%, which you might need to do if you're living in a larger metropolitan area. Remember to add utility, parking, and insurance costs to your rent when you're figuring The Number out.

If you own your own home, you'll have some additional costs to consider beyond the mortgage payment. Property taxes, insurance, utilities, and maintenance are all part of the home-ownership price tag. With fewer people paying the overhead, can you afford to stay put?

VICTORIA'S STORY

Here were my costs for living in a three-bedroom house in the country in 2015:

Mortgage payment/rent: $0

Taxes: $2,677

Heating/hydro/firewood: $3,166

Insurance: $924

Repairs: $3,240

Water system: $378

Planned replacements: $675

Total: $11,060 for the year or $922 a month

All of this is after paying for the house! And because I live a one-hour walk from the closest store where I can buy milk, a car is a necessity, so it adds more money to my costs.

Knowing your budget numbers lets you clearly see if you can afford to stay where you are now or if you need to start planning a move. For all the people who rail at the idea of allocating $300 to $400 a month to home maintenance, know that homes get older, wear out, and need some fixing up. If you don't plan for home maintenance, then everything that must be fixed becomes an emergency.

GAIL'S STORY
. . . .

I planned for two years to do a gentle kitchen reno: new melamine counter-tops, new tap and sink, new hardware for the cupboards and drawers, new backsplash. The job came in on budget and I was pleased with the result. Then a pipe leaked and my basement ceiling had to be replaced. My shower fixtures wore out—thank you, hard water—and I had to have the cartridges replaced. My shower started to leak. The toilets had to be replaced. The microwave blew up (nothing I did). Even the valve for the water coming from the town into my home started to leak. It was everything all at once. Thank heavens I take my own advice and had a healthy home maintenance fund at the ready. By the time everything was fixed, my well-planned $6,000 renovation had expanded to over $18,000 in repairs.

You can't honestly say you never expected your roof to wear out. So pretending it will never happen won't get you the money you need to make the fix when the time comes. Better to set aside money every month so that when something has to be updated or replaced, you can do it without squeezing your cash flow.

After considering all your costs, you may decide you cannot afford your current location. Running it with two adults may have worked, but on your lonesome the cost to your cash flow is just too high.

Ready to figure out how much of your budget is going to your shelter costs?

Make a list of all the things associated with keeping a roof over your head. Look back over the last year to see what your average monthly costs were. No guessing!

Mortgage payment/rent:

Taxes:

Heating/hydro/firewood:

Insurance:

Repairs:

Water system:

Replacements:

Total:

Take your total, divide it by your monthly take-home income, and then multiply by 100. That'll give you a percentage. Again, look back at your last tax return or use your bank statements to find your average monthly take-home.

If your total monthly shelter costs were $1,749 and your average monthly income was $4,067, the math would look like this:

1749 ÷ 4067 x 100 = 43%

Remember the rule of thumb: you should be spending about 35% of your take-home pay on shelter, unless you have no consumer debt. With no debt payments, you have another 15% available in your cash flow to spend any way you want. That means you can choose to allocate up to 50% of your resources to shelter as long as everything else in your budget is in line.

WAYS TO MAKE STAYING WORK

If you decide you want to stay in your home but there are some hurdles to get over to make it work, that's okay. You just have to get creative to come up with ways to make staying possible. Perhaps you think being in a house on your own (or with young kids) is just going to be too much work. Maybe you're worried about being lonely. Maybe you're concerned about not having enough money to do all the other things you want to do. Each of these problems has a solution or three; you just have to put on your thinking cap.

TOO MUCH WORK, NOT ENOUGH TIME

Living in your own home is nothing like renting. If you rent and your fridge breaks down, it's your landlord's job to pay to have it fixed. But when you own, you're not just CEO of Everything, you're also the Janitor. When something needs to be cleaned, repaired, or replaced, it's up to you to make it happen.

If you love your home but worry about the work it requires, you can hire out the things you don't want to do or don't have time to do, as long as you have enough money or the right friends.

GAIL'S STORY

I turned the area around the house from lawn to perennial garden. I hated the grass and had always wanted a cottage garden, so I made one. And then came the weeding. I set myself a limit of one bucket of weeds a day. Weeding is great exercise, and I find it meditative. When the weeds are more than I can handle, I hire a teenager to weed for me. I pay her $15 an hour, and she's happy to put in three hours a week helping me stay ahead of the weeds.

Gardens have a way of sprouting and expanding. One day you may realize your hobby is now a pain in the ass and you no longer want the responsibility of maintaining Eden. But that doesn't mean you have to sell and move. If you love where you live, you just have to find a way to make your garden less work. You can hire someone to take on the heavy lifting: weeding, cutting the lawn, trimming the hedges. You can revamp your garden to minimize the work. If you xeriscape, you won't even have to water.

Cleaning out eavestroughs, washing windows, and repainting are all things you can hire out if the thought of climbing a ladder makes you shudder.

GAIL'S STORY

Vivi lives in a beautiful home. But it's a lot of house for one chick, particularly since Vivi is now in her mid-60s. So Vivi decided to rent out part of her home to a lovely couple named Darren and Marta. For a reduced rent,

Marta does the heavy cleaning, and Darren, who is a very handy fellow, keeps the property shipshape for Vivi.

The point is to enjoy being a homeowner, not to feel crushed by the duties. If you have a hectic schedule—a demanding work life, kids with lots of activities, a busy travel schedule—you might decide to swap ownership for renting to make things easier, assuming you can find what you want to rent at a reasonable price. CEOs weigh costs against benefits all the time. They examine alternatives. As CEO of Everything, if you want to stay where you are, you need only come up with alternatives to make it so. And if you find that staying is more work than it's worth, you'll be ready to embrace the alternative.

I JUST DON'T WANT TO BE LONELY

Don't like the idea of living alone? Worried about having to live with someone else? Feel caught between a rock and a hard place?

There are all kinds of ways to live together so you aren't lonely. You can co-purchase a duplex with a friend or relative so you each have your own space but are close enough to check in on each other. You can turn the basement of your existing home into a separate apartment so you can have someone living close by who is willing to share some of the tasks, like gardening and snow shovelling. You can house-share with friends who have a home in a warmer climate: they live with you in the summer, you live with them in the winter when you want to escape the snow. You can take in a student who will only be there for part of the year.

I am considering the idea of getting a house with a rental apartment in it. I'd have a student live with me during the school term (September to May), giving me the summers with my own space. Having a rental unit means valuable tax writeoffs. I've also been talking with friends about the idea of sharing space in the future, and I'm open to finding someone who wants to buy a duplex with me.

The benefit of knowing the person you are sharing space with or have proximity to means you can share meals, look after each other's plants, and pet sit. You can share a car, a washer and dryer, and the luggage. Sharing space with your sibling, with your adult children, with your best friend's daughter who is going to college where you live, is a great way to split costs, enjoy company, and feel safe.

VICTORIA'S STORY

Nina and Olivia are sisters who sold their individual houses and bought a large two-level home. Each floor has its own entry and is a self-contained apartment. The sisters have cats that don't get along and this plan helped keep the peace. This new home allowed each of them to access some of their capital so they could do more travelling.

If you're used to living on your own, it may take some time to get used to a new living arrangement. Be patient. And make sure you establish the ground rules from the get-go.

If you do end up sharing and can't stand dirty dishes in the sink, say so. Allergic to perfume? Say so. Make it clear when you expect the other person to hand over their share of the money, who will clean what and when, and what you each need in terms of privacy and quiet. How do you feel about sleepover guests? Are pets allowed? Suppose you want to throw a party?

GAIL'S STORY

When Tammy and her husband divorced, Tammy didn't have the money to buy him out. She wanted to keep her two kids in the neighbourhood but couldn't find a place she could afford that suited them. Tammy's sister, Tara, decided to buy the other half of the house from Tammy's ex. Tara turned the second floor into her living space, while Tammy and the kids moved their bedrooms into the basement. They agreed to share the kitchen and family room on the main floor. Tara had her own space upstairs, so when she "entertained," the kids sleeping in the basement weren't disturbed. Tammy was thrilled to have the company, and Tara was delighted to be part of her nieces' lives.

KIDS MOVING HOME

Sometimes the decision to stay involves a kid offering to move back in. It seems like a good short-term solution. You need company and help around the house. It allows you to stay in the family home. Everyone saves money.

You need to be aware of how other siblings may feel about the arrangement; you must make sure everyone understands this is in YOUR best interest. As long as this is working for you, it's a good arrangement. If it becomes a problem for you, then you'll need to make other plans.

If at some point down the road, you and your child deem that joint signing privileges on your bank account is a good idea, you must make this transparent to all your other children. Resentment builds quickly between sibs when one thinks another is getting preferential treatment. While you might like to think sibling rivalry was left on the grade-six playground, it is alive and well and living in 50-year-old siblings. When money is involved, issues of abuse and subterfuge rear their ugly heads.

It may be hard to hear that your child may not have your best interest at heart. It happens more often than people think. Your daughter wants a new flat-screen television for her room. Done. Your son thinks a cleaning lady to keep the house tidy is a good idea. Done. Cellphone bills move on to one family plan, which you pay. Darling daughter thinks, since she's driving you around, you should buy a new car. Oh, and can I please borrow $5,000?

If you don't want to be a statistic, don't be a sucker. Your grown children are adults and have the responsibility to stand on their own two feet. If you decide you will live together, make sure you both know the ground rules from the get-go. Who will pay the utilities? Who will buy the groceries? Who will clean the bathroom?

GAIL'S STORY

When Darlene's husband died, she was lost. She started talking about selling the family home, but her children tried to talk her out of it. Darlene told them the house was too big for her and she'd be lonely. Besides, she didn't drive, so getting around was too hard. That's when her son, Markus, suggested he move back in. He'd pay the utilities and do the maintenance on the house as his "rent." That would let him save for a down payment of his own. Darlene didn't mind making his meals and doing his laundry. Markus's sister, Julie, thought he was getting a sweet deal, until he pointed out that the alternative would be for Julie to take Darlene grocery shopping every week. This upfront discussion set the tone for the deal everyone agreed to.

I CAN'T AFFORD MY HOME ANYMORE

Many of the solutions to being lonely also apply to finding a way to afford a home you want to stay in. From renting a part of your home to living *Golden Girls*–style with friends who pay you rent, thinking outside the box can keep you in your home. Host an international student if you live close to colleges or universities. Turn your beautiful home into a bed and breakfast or create a space you can use as a short-term rental, using services like airbnb.ca and roomorama.com.

GAIL'S STORY

I had a director who bought a home with an attic apartment. He didn't want anyone living upstairs permanently, particularly in the summer when he wanted to use the deck. But he liked the idea of renting out the space on Airbnb from time to time to generate a little extra income. The rate of $130 a night eliminated any riff-raff, and he earned enough in just a few nights a month to pay for an annual vacation.

CAN I AFFORD TO BUY ON MY OWN?

While renting may have been your first choice of accommodation when you just started out or your circumstances first changed, think about whether you still enjoy renting. Or has your temporary plan turned into a more permanent solution because you think it takes two to own?

Watching friends partner up and buy homes with the benefit of two incomes may leave you wondering if it is even possible for you to buy on your own. Time to go back to the budget.

VICTORIA'S STORY
• •
After a fight with my landlady, I began crunching the numbers because it became clear I needed to stop renting. I bought my first home, a semi-detached duplex, just months later. In the end I became a homeowner and a landlady all in one shot. Risky? Yes. Rewarding? Definitely.

You may decide to buy a rental property (hey, you were a great tenant) as a method of reducing your costs and having someone help you pay off the mortgage. Maybe you'll move from a rental apartment to a condominium, since you don't want all the work of a house. Property-wise, you can do anything your imagination and budget will allow.

To see if homeownership will work for you without squeezing your budget tighter than a nun's knees, practise living as if you have already bought. Here's how:

First, figure out what kind of property you want to buy and what you'll spend. Then add together your housing costs. This will include your mortgage payments, property taxes, condo and maintenance fees, utilities, and home insurance. That number—that big number—is what you'll have to come up with every single month if you buy that property.

The next step is to subtract whatever you're currently paying for shelter from that big number. The difference between what you're paying now and what you're going to have to fork out when you buy must go into a savings account every month for at least six months so you can prove to yourself your costs are manageable. This isn't a theoretical exercise. You actually have to take the difference and sock it away every month for at least six months before you buy.

This will achieve two things:

1. It will teach you to live on less disposable income. You better start practising before you buy so you're ready for the adjustment in your lifestyle when you do take the big step. Loads of people buy a home and then keep on spending like they did before they became homeowners, racking up gobs of debt.
2. It will help you build your down payment.

Home ownership isn't for everyone. Some folks are happier and better off renting. There's nothing wrong with that choice. And don't fall for the crap that you're throwing your life and money away. Just point out that of your best friend's $2,100-a-month mortgage payment, $2,084 is going to interest, at least for the first few years.

Peace of mind, ease of movement, and a sense of balance are all important things to have, too. And homeownership as an investment isn't a sure thing, no matter what the experts (or your family) say. Homeownership does bring the opportunity to grow equity over time, but if you rent and invest wisely, you can achieve much the same end.

MOVING ON

If you want to escape old memories, if your home feels like an empty nest, if moving closer to family lets you see them more often, then it may be time to pack and go. Maybe you want to get at the equity you've built up. Maybe the house is just too big; you rattle around and don't use half the rooms. You don't want the bother of all the upkeep. The gardens used to be great, but now they're too much work. The neighbourhood has changed. You just can't manage all the stairs anymore. Hey, there are dozens of good reasons to move. The most important is that you want to.

If your adult kids object to you selling "their home," a quick end to the discussion is to ask the question "Terrific, you'd like to buy it, then?" If they don't want to pony up the pesos, put it on the market.

Once you've made the decision to sell, you'll have to choose whether you will rent or buy again.

Renting puts upkeep and repairs in someone else's court. Renting gives you a certain financial stability, since your costs are fixed, with only small increases each year. Renting lets you pick up and leave for a vacation by simply closing the door behind you. Renting gives you the option to change your mind and move to another location with minimum costs.

Ownership gives you more flexibility to make your home just the way you want it by painting, changing flooring, even moving (or removing) walls. And if markets go up, you'll build equity. Downsizing means money in your pocket from the equity you built up in your previous home and from your reduced carrying costs. But downsizing also means you'll have to get rid of the stuff that won't fit in your new, smaller space.

CHOOSING THE NEXT PLACE TO LIVE

When it comes to deciding where you'll next hang your hat, many factors have to be considered, from how long you plan to live there, to where you'll look for a new home, to whom you'll choose to live with.

How long you will live there? Is this an in-between move, something temporary, or do you plan to stay until they carry you away in a box? Think about your time frame. Buy only if you plan to remain in the same place for seven years or more. That's about how long it takes to average your moving costs (sales commission, taxes, legal fees, and the like) to a reasonable amount. Will you have to move again at retirement, or will your new place accommodate your changing physical needs? Can you see yourself still comfortable there in 10 or 20 years?

Are you a city mouse or a country mouse? Living in a city comes with advantages like transportation options, choices of restaurants and shops, and access to more people. Living in the country puts you closer to nature, is much quieter, and often gets you more home for your money. Think about the trade-offs:

- Do you prefer the convenience of walking to everything or are you fine with driving a half-hour to get to a store?
- Do you prefer the sound of crickets or the buzz of city nightlife?
- Would you rather have access to public transportation or drive yourself?
- Do you like going to plays, lectures, and restaurants or do you love to spend time on solo activities like reading or knitting?
- Are you happy cooking for yourself or would you rather eat takeout?
- Do you still need to work or are you living on a fixed income?
- Are you worried about the level of crime around you or do you feel safe?
- Are you sick of traffic or do you hate the idea of being isolated?
- Do you wish you could see the stars or do you put more stock in being able to get a copy of the *New York Times* on Sunday?
- Do you need access to high-speed internet or will you make do with whatever you can get?

Often it comes down to stimulation and convenience versus quiet, solitude, and beautiful surroundings. Maybe you'll compromise by choosing to live within a reasonable drive of a large city so you can partake in the benefits of city life when you want but revel in the joys of country living the rest of the time.

If you've never lived in the country or in a smaller town, try it on before making the big move. Rent a place for a few weeks to see if you are suited to the pace and lifestyle. Ditto for moving to the city. Take a short-term rental and live like a local for a few weeks to see how it fits.

GAIL'S STORY

I've lived downtown in a big city and I've lived in the bush. I can live anywhere. The only place I swore I'd never live was in a small town. Too much busybody behaviour. I despise the cliques. And don't even get me started on small-town politics. But as with just about everything else in my life, whenever I say, "I'll never!" the universe conspires to make me. When it came time for my last move, I was living in the bush with a bunch of critters and a half-hour commute one-way to get the kids to school. That clearly was not going to work, since I had to be on the road two days a week for my job. Without my ex, I couldn't make country life work. So I moved to a small town. At the time, there were no other options. I had to get my daughter close enough to school that she could cope when I was away. And I had to stay close enough to my ex for us to share joint custody of my son. So I bought a house in a small town. There, universe, you've had your way with me again! And, by the way, I was right: I can live anywhere.

Do you want to live with family? Combined family living can be a wonderful experience or it can be a nightmare. While the idea of a multi-generational family is often touted as something from "the good old days," there are some key issues you should consider before bringing a bunch of relatives under the same roof.

First, think about how well you get along. Looking back over your relationship with your mother, your son and your daughter-in-law, or your sister, how have you gotten on? Don't whitewash what has been a sticky relationship just because you think amalgamating the family is your best next step. While all families come with conflict, if you have never really gotten along, don't expect a magical change in the relationship. You'll only be disappointed.

If you not only love each other but like each other, the next step will be to lay the ground rules for a happy co-existence. What are the rules of the house, and is everyone happy to live with them? If you go to bed at 9 p.m. and your sister likes to watch television until 2 a.m., how will you reconcile your early-bird/night-owl schedules? How will your children feel when they see you cuddling on the couch with your new main squeeze? If you're living with your grandbabies, are you willing to be considered a built-in babysitter? How will your deeply religious values conflict with teenager in-your-face outspokenness?

If you're going to fight over the pop cans left in the living room, what to make for dinner, or how often to take out the garbage, cohabitation will not work. Best to know what's very important and what's totally aggravating right off the bat. Talk about things like space and privacy issues, your personal values, your need for order and cleanliness, and who's going to walk the dog on the daily before you start packing.

Don't avoid the financial chat. It's easier to say, "Oh, we'll figure that out down the road." Figure it out first. Everyone should know what's expected financially before you take the big step of commingling your lives. Will the person moving in contribute financially to the household? If so, how much? If the home must be modified, who will pay for that? Will each of you maintain your financial privacy or is family money up for discussion? Are there services you want that you're willing to pay for yourself? Who will be responsible for what bills? How do you feel about being tapped for a loan?

GAIL'S STORY
· ·

I have neighbours who have a grown daughter living with them. She's self-employed, and living with her parents gives her some financial flexibility, particularly in less profitable months. They spend the winter in a warmer climate with the peace of mind of knowing their home is in good hands. They even have matching dogs! The situation works for everyone.

After the shock of a death or a divorce, it's perfectly reasonable to want to cling to family. But independence shouldn't be the thing you sacrifice because you choose to live with family. You need to have your own stories to share about what you are doing. If you just glom on to the family and their stories, you will become boring. If you make your life small, you become boring. There is too much to do and see and learn about in this great big world. Be a good role model to your children and grandchildren; show them how willing you are to embrace what comes next in your life.

WHAT WILL IT COST TO MOVE?

Gone are the days of pizza and beer and a few friends throwing your stuff in a van. When most established households move, there's a moving company involved. There are also some considerable costs associated with switching homes, when the switch involves the sale and repurchase of a home.

Let's say you decide to sell your $500,000 house to downgrade to a $275,000 home so you can pocket some equity. Assuming you use a real estate agent, you'll pay a commission, usually 5%, which works out to $25,000. You could, of course, do the legwork yourself, but you'd have to be prepared for the calls from agents and the time it takes to advertise and show your home. Don't forget that there's HST (or other provincial or territorial taxes) on the agent's commission ($3,250).

You may have to spend some money fixing up your home before you sell. It is a lot easier to sell a house that's attractive; that may mean putting some dollars into making sure everything is clean and neat, and ensuring small defects have been fixed. Anticipate spending anywhere from $5,000 to $20,000 fixing and staging to make the sale.

If your home has major structural defects, you will have to decide if you'll fix what's broken or if you'll lower the price to sell as is. It comes down to the math. If you'll gain your money back, do the fixes. If you can sell and negotiate the cost of the repair out of the sale price, that can be easier on you. Don't know what shape your house is in? Get your own home inspection done. That way, you'll not only know what the buyer will come back with, but you'll also have an estimate for the cost of repairs, so you'll be working from a place of knowledge. Be prepared to negotiate.

GAIL'S STORY

When I was buying my last home, it was clear that the roof would have to be replaced PDQ. So I negotiated the cost of the new roof off the price of the house and banked the diff for that spring, when I'd pay the roof monkeys to swing their hammers. The seller was happy enough not to have to deal with a roof replacement in December.

Do you still have a mortgage? If you're breaking your mortgage contract, there's a fee for that. An interest rate penalty, sometimes called an LIC (lost interest compensation) or an IRD (interest rate differential), is the fee the lender charges you for breaking the mortgage early. Hey, a deal is a deal, and if you break the deal you shouldn't be surprised that you have to pay. Sometimes it's three months' worth of interest. Sometimes it's much worse. If you can take your mortgage to your new home—which is called "porting your mortgage"—you'll just have to pay the porting fee. And if you're discharging your mortgage, expect to pay a fee of about $300.

If you live in a rural area, you'll have to provide a certificate for your well and another for your septic system. You may also be asked to provide a survey to show how your property sits on the land and whether there are any encroachments. You may still have your survey from when you bought, but if you don't, you'll have to pay to get another.

And, of course, there are legal fees. People like to "forget" about the $600 to $900 in legal fees and the $300 or so in disbursements, even though we know that we're going to need a lawyer to close the deal. Go with a lawyer who makes their living closing real estate transactions because they'll have streamlined the system and you'll pay less.

Then there are the fees to buy your new home. Land transfer tax will easily be your biggest expense. The tax is based on a percentage of the purchase price of the home, and it varies from province to province.

Most people who have never bought before have no idea what the "property tax adjustment" cost is all about. If you're buying a home from George, and he's already paid property taxes on the house for months you'll be living in it, you've got to pay George back for the money he's already sent in. You're responsible for the property taxes from the date you take possession, and this is calculated by the lawyer and paid back to the seller as part of the transaction.

Another cost that throws buyers is the "interest adjustment date." The maximum this can be is one month's worth of interest, but most often it is less. If your mortgage is advanced (sent to the lawyer to pay to the seller) on June 14, you'll owe interest from that date until the date your first mortgage payment comes out of the bank (likely July 1). It's a good idea to ask your lender to calculate your interest adjustment so you know what to expect.

As with selling, there will be legal fees ($1,000), home inspection fees ($500), and, if you're getting a new mortgage, a home appraisal fee ($300). You might also decide to buy title insurance ($500), which can protect you from a loss because of unknown title defects, existing liens, encroachment issues, title fraud, and errors in surveys.

Then there are the actual moving costs. Someone comes in and does an estimate of how much all of your stuff weighs. If ever there was a great time to downsize your stuff, it is before the estimator comes in. Do you want the moving company to pack and move all your goods? If so, you pay for boxes, tape, and the hourly wage of the packers who arrive the day before the move. Or you can pack yourself and just have the strong men and women come in and move your stuff.

VICTORIA'S STORY
. . . .
On the day of my last move, when the driver arrived he asked for a cheque for almost $4,500 before anything was loaded. Make sure you know what the costs involved in moving are before you even start packing.

You also pay for services to be disconnected and reconnected. Bottom line: moving is expensive, so know the costs and think carefully before you move. And moving is stressful, so make sure you have a plan to keep the wheels turning as smoothly as possible.

I'd labelled the boxes and tried to put a few notes about the contents on the outside. Unpacking 10 or 20 boxes labelled "kitchen" meant I found my mixer long before I found something useful like a plate. For my next move, I plan to pack a box of essentials and take it in my car. I'll include cleaning products, a few dishes, glasses, cutlery, knife, cutting board, two pots, corkscrew, napkins, a set of sheets, pillow, duvet, and the bathroom essentials.

Putting a "for sale" sign on your home can be a tough decision. But as CEO of Everything, you're going to have to make tough decisions. The point isn't to hold on desperately to what you had; the point is to figure out what you want and make that your new reality.

The decision to stay or move on isn't one to be taken lightly or to be made quickly. Even if your financial situation warrants immediate action, you're better off finding a short-term solution (like taking in a roomie) unless you absolutely must move quickly to avoid further trouble.

Take your time. Decisions made while you're still in the throes of grieving can come back to haunt you. So don't rush into anything. If you can, give yourself about six months before you make major financial decisions like selling your home.

The decision to stay or go will be both emotional and logical. DO NOT let the emotional overrule your logic. Yes, you may feel attached to *that* place but, in the end, a home is anywhere you live with joy.

9 · PAY IT FORWARD

Death, divorce, and the disruptions of life may have made you feel like you were looking at the end of your dreams. But now that you're setting new goals and dreaming new dreams you know that change may bend you, but it doesn't break you. Change gives you the opportunity to discard what's old and unnecessary to make space for the new and exciting.

You might be the first of your peer group to get a divorce. Or you may have been widowed earlier than your friends. Going first was hard because very few rules were in place. You had to learn as you went, tripping and falling, getting up and putting yourself back on track. How much easier would it have been if you had had a guide?

Now you can be that guide.

VICTORIA'S STORY

Sometimes all I had to do for friends who had recently buried a mate was listen. I got really good at listening. I would sit, being completely present with them, giving them the space to tell me what they'd lost, what they were remembering, what they needed to tell of their story. People grieving are looking for validation, for reassurance that what they're missing is worth my time listening. I'm honoured to be able to share those memories with them.

As you trim away the old parts of the life that no longer works for you and stitch together a new, better fitting life, others are watching. When family, friends, or co-workers are plunged into a new schema, you can empathize and share your experiences.

Hand the person who is divorced or widowed this book. But don't stop there. Your experience—what you learned from going through it yourself—can help someone who may falter in finding their feet. You can make the path so much easier for someone else by turning your hard-won wisdom into practical help.

You have, after all, done it. You've made it through your own crisis to become CEO of Everything. You embody a lot of learning. And like so many CEOs before you, now you're ready to play the role of mentor.

Be patient. You know that when your world was turned upside down and sideways you needed time to right yourself. You also know what someone says and does during a crisis may seem extremely out of character. Remember when you were acting like a crazy person? Your patience, understanding, and guidance can help your friend regain their equilibrium.

GAIL'S STORY
• •
My girlfriend—we'll call her Alice—came over to my house one day to cry

her heart out. (Alice and I are crying buddies.) Alice had just realized that many of the things she had been planning for her life weren't going to happen. "So now that he's left me, what's this all been for?" she wailed, as I poured her a cup of tea and handed her the box of tissues. "I mean, seriously, why am I even bothering? I feel like I'm stuck."

"Let's leave out all the things that come with mating and mommying," I said. "Tell me what else you'd want to make your life a little sweeter?"

That damn girl couldn't think of a thing. Ninety percent of the time Alice was thrilled with the life she had. It was only when she got to thinking about the life she could have had that she made herself miserable.

I listened to Alice sob and heave and when there was some space, I asked, "So, tell me again what it is you thought your life was going to be like." Alice described it in great detail. "That sounds like a pretty perfect life," I said. She acknowledged that it was. "Y'know, no one gets that, right?" She looked over at me a little surprised. "Seriously, no one gets that. You've seen my life, right?" She nodded, a small smile coming to her face. "And I'm pretty thrilled with my messed-up, mucked-up life." Now she was grinning.

"So what is it that you like about your life right now?" She started slowly, finding it hard to see anything good, so I had to point out a couple of things, like her freedom to travel and her spotless apartment. Then she got on a roll.

Offer your help. It's not enough to want to help; you must explicitly tell your friend, your workmate, your neighbour that you are there to help. People in crisis often can't hear hints, so be overt in your offers. Say, "I have your back."

Be ready to listen. Reassure your pal that they may cry, yell, laugh, ramble, or be silent. It's normal. You've seen it. You've done it. And then make sure you listen more than you talk. As your CEO protege sorts through thoughts and feelings, stay open and ready to hear them. Skip phrases like "You'll bounce back soon" or "I know how you feel." Remember how much they irritated you?

Don't take sides. While it's fine to affirm the person has a right to feel as they do, don't get into the emotional swim. You might think that your friend wants your support in the form of spewing nasties at their mate, but it isn't productive. Stay neutral while you listen. Acknowledge that the situation is a difficult one without trying to lay blame.

GAIL'S STORY

When I was going through my last breakup, I called Brownie to rant and rave about my ex. God bless the woman, she listened to me wail and cry, hiss and spit. Just being able to vent to someone I knew would never hold it against me (or for that matter, him) was such a relief.

Take one day at a time. Remind the newly promoted CEO of Everything to relax. There will be a lot to do, but thinking of it all at once can be overwhelming. Help them make a list of what they will do today. Make a list for tomorrow. Routines help to keep life moving, so encourage your friend to develop some new ones that fit their new life.

Watch out for the children. While your friend may be mourning the loss of a significant part of their life, their children will also be in mourning. Think about how confusing death or divorce must be to kids. You can reassure them that they are safe and still cared for. Be a presence in their lives. Establish a new routine specifically with you. Throw a ball once a week. Email jokes. Invite them over to make lunch. Notice and remark on what they are wearing. Ask questions about their day, their friends, their favourite activities. Let them know you see them. They exist for you and you are glad they are in the world. Say it out loud.

Help with chores. Remember when someone showed up at your door with pasta salad or a roast chicken? Your friend won't remember to eat, can't be bothered to cook, doesn't have an appetite. Bring over something fresh and something for the freezer the next time you get together. Offer to do the laundry, cut the grass, or change the beds. If your friend is feeling isolated, having your company while you do these small tasks will make a world of difference. You're not responsible for making your friend "better" or speeding them through the process. You're just there to provide loving support.

Share your journey. No matter how uncertain, incompetent, or helpless your friend may feel, they do not want your pity. Instead, tap into your own experiences to connect with them. Share how you felt, what you did, and how you struggled to show them that they are not alone in experiencing the feelings they have. You want them to know that you survived and so will they. Avoid pep talks. This sharing has to be genuine.

Include them in social events. Reassure them that it is fine to make plans and then change them. Every plan they make with you comes equipped with an escape hatch, so there's no need to say sorry, only that it won't work out today. Buy two tickets to the next event you want to attend. Encourage them to take those first shaky steps out again. Offer to be their plus-one to events they may be attending.

Share your life. Tell your friend about your mundane life. They need to know things are continuing on in the larger world. This also provides relief from the intensity of their situation. If you can, tell a funny story so they can laugh.

Offer to drive. It sounds funny, but when anyone becomes single they must do all the driving. It feels great when someone else takes the wheel and chauffeurs. And it is one less thing the new CEO has to think about.

Don't patronize. Don't say things like "Snap out of it" or "It didn't take me this long to get back to life" or "Wow! I don't know how you do it." Your friend's emotions will be raw. They may feel overwhelmed. They don't need to feel judged.

VICTORIA'S STORY

After becoming a widow, someone gave me a gift certificate for a massage. When I arrived, the masseuse asked the usual "How are you?" I replied that I was coping. "You are a tough one," she said. Tough? I could barely drive. It had taken all my effort to just get there. Don't be one of those people who speaks without thinking.

Ask for directions. Does your friend want you to check in on how they're doing each time you see them? Or would they rather you go about your relationship without putting the death or divorce front and centre? Do they need help sorting out the estate? Would they like recommendations on experts like accountants, lawyers, or financial advisors? Suggest your friend make a list, and add to that list, whenever anything pops into their head. Then they can help you help them.

Remind them they're awesome. Being widowed or divorced makes a person feel like the rug has been pulled right out from under them. Having lived it, you know that. You also know how important it was to you when people reminded you how gorgeous, smart, funny, charming, or loved you were. Pay it forward.

Stay connected. Divorces can drag on. Widowhood isn't something you get over in a few months or even a few years. While it may look like dude has his life firmly in hand, don't assume he is fixed and move on. Check in to see how he's doing. "So, it's been a while now. How are you feeling about being CEO of Everything?" Remember that the holidays can be a particularly tough time. Offer to share your holiday magic.

You may have started out in your role as CEO on shaky legs, but eventually you transitioned from others helping to carry you to you holding yourself up. Now you have enough strength to help carry another. You have the experiences. You have a model. Off you go!

FINAL THOUGHTS

When you started on the journey to becoming CEO of Everything, you might not have realized just how capable you were of taking on this job. It's a big title. It comes with big responsibilities. While your tendency may be to criticize yourself for not moving quickly enough, not being decisive enough, not being adept enough, don't.

You are a student of being single. You are doing an apprenticeship in living on your own. No one gains mastery instantly. Day by day you will build your experience and knowledge until you are confident and content.

CEOs claim the skill of resilience and the ability to take a punch and get back up. You will learn to deal with disappointments and setbacks, as well as to savour the triumph of a job well done.

Where you are now isn't where you started, and you're not done yet. You will continue to evolve until the title of CEO fits you like your most comfortable pair of shoes. You'll look back and smile at how far you've come. You'll look forward, sometimes with excitement, sometimes with trepidation, but always with the knowledge that whatever life throws at you, you've got it.

Knowing yourself is an important part of being a successful CEO. When you know yourself, you can be confident that you're ready to meet whatever challenges show up to the party. Learn what routines support you and your goals. Figure out what gets in your way. Be greedy for a greater understanding of yourself and ways to improve. Having explored the options for how you'll move forward while reading this book, you now know being able to see alternatives provides you with the greatest range of choices.

CEOs live and die on their ability to focus their resources. Your resources include your time, your money, and your thoughts. Be conscious of how you're spending your time. Watch where your money goes. And be aware of your thoughts; they can take you down dark alleyways or into meadows of sunlight. Your thoughts are yours to control.

If you've ever said, "I used to think," you know how to change your mind. Maybe you said, "I used to think I would not make it as a single person" or "I used to think I would never be able to afford to buy a home on my own." Now you feel better equipped and able to update your thinking. When you get more information, you make more informed decisions and choices that are better suited to you.

Everyone changes. Imagine the tattoos you would have got at 19. Would they be the same tattoos you would get at 49?

Being capable, in charge, and joyful doesn't mean that you'll never get lonely. Even people who are in long and happy relationships get lonely sometimes. You may fantasize about someone who'll take care of you. It's normal. No one starts as a fully formed CEO. You grow into the role.

Ultimately, being CEO of Everything means you must answer the question "Am I pleased with my life?" If you're making the decisions, if you're choosing what to do each day, if you're moving in the direction you want, you should be pleased.

Once you take on the role of CEO, you'll find that self-determination is addictive. While you may have gone into singleness thinking that living alone was just one of your options, you may decide it's your best option. Having grown accustomed to your own way of doing things, you may want to keep things just as they are. When you create a life in which your needs and wants are satisfied, you may be very content embracing your single status.

You will continue to change. Your life is still unfolding. You may surprise yourself as you layer new memories on top of old. One day you may forget your anniversary. The date no longer triggers a sense of loss because you've overwritten that memory with new ones. And so it will go until what was is replaced by what is and the hopes of what will be.

You reign as CEO of a life of your own making. Comfortable alone or with others, laughing or listening, contemplative or dancing with joy, you embrace all aspects of YOU with unconditional love.

Congratulations! You are CEO of Everything.

APPENDICES
Appendix 1: Divorce Petition Checklist

Here are questions you're going to need to answer at some point in your divorce. You might as well get started thinking about them now. Your lawyer may have more, but these will get you off to a good start.

ABOUT THE KIDS

Who will be the custodial or residential parent?

What rights will the other parent have in terms of being with the children?

Who will pay transportation expenses incurred if the kids must travel?

Will there be any restriction on where the custodial or residential parent may move with the children?

How will major decisions affecting the children's health, welfare, and education be made?

ABOUT YOUR HOME

If You Own Your Home

Will your home be sold? Will one of the parties deed his or her interest to the other?

Will one of the parties have the right to continue to live in the home, and if so, for how long?

Will he or she have the right to rent any portion of the home or to allow any other person to live there?

If rent will be received, who will have the right to keep it?

Will that right be affected by remarriage or living in a common-law relationship?

If the home is to be sold either now or in the future, how will the proceeds be split?

If the parties cannot agree on the provisions of the sale (e.g., the selling price, private sale, or multiple listing), how will this be determined?

Who will be responsible for the ordinary maintenance and carrying charges on the home until it is sold?

Who will be responsible for major repairs and the costs of preparing the home for sale?

If and when the home is to be sold, will either party have a first option to buy it?

Who will be responsible for any taxes, if applicable?

If You Rent Your Home

Who will have the right to continue to live in the home?

Who must pay the rent and other carrying charges in the future?

How will security deposits be split?

Will the departing spouse be obliged to help the remaining spouse in renewing the lease if the landlord will not renew it without his or her signature?

ABOUT WHAT YOU OWE

What personal debts (not including business loans and the home mortgage) do parties have?

Who will be responsible for paying each of these debts?

ABOUT WHAT YOU OWN

How will the furniture, household furnishings, and other items of personal property in the marital residence be split?

How will money in savings or chequing accounts in either the joint or individual names of the parties be split?

How will investments such as stocks, bonds, or other securities in either the joint or individual names of the parties be split?

How will items such as cars, boats, motorcycles, or other items of personal property in either the joint or individual names of the parties be split?

To what extent will the parties have the right to share in any pension or retirement benefits to which the other is or may be entitled?

To what extent will one party have the right to a share in the value of any business, professional practice, royalties, or other personal property owned by the other party?

ABOUT SUPPORT

Will either party be required to financially support the other? If so, how much and for how long?

Will either party be required to pay support to the other spouse for the children? If so, how much and for how long?

If there is more than one child, by how much will the child-support payments be reduced when the obligation for the support of one or more of the children ends?

Will the support payments change in the future to reflect changes in financial circumstances of either of the parties, economic conditions, or other factors?

Who will be entitled to claim the children as exemptions for income tax purposes?

Will either or both parties be obligated to pay for the children's post-secondary education? If so, which expenses, and to what extent?

If those expenses are financed, who will be responsible for repayment?

Will there be any reduction in support payments while children are attending a post-secondary institution?

ABOUT INSURANCE

Will either party be obligated to maintain life insurance a) for the benefit of the other, and if so, in what amount and for how long? b) for the benefit of the children, and if so, in what amount and for how long? Who will be the beneficiary of such insurance?

Will the obligation to maintain life insurance decrease (as to amount) in the future, and if so, when and in what amount?

Will either party be obligated to provide medical or other
insurance a) for the benefit of the other? For how long? b)
for the benefit of the children? For how long?

Who will be responsible for paying the children's medical,
dental, drug, or hospital expenses that are not reimbursed
by any insurance that either of the parties may have?

Appendix 2: Who Do You Have to Notify?

Here is a partial list of places/accounts/holdings you will need
to notify, update, and provide with new paperwork (such as a
death certificate or insurance documents):

Credit card companies

Will

Bank accounts

Trust accounts

Joint accounts

Beneficiary designations

Annuities

RRSPs and RRIFs

Pensions

Loans or lines of credit, especially anything you co-signed

Insurance (life, disability, home, car, cottage, jewellery)

Utility companies, such as hydro, electricity, phone, and
water

Magazine subscription renewals

Cable TV or satellite TV

Internet

Cellphone

Everything at your place of employment, especially contact names and beneficiaries

Signing authorities

Everything at school if you have kids

Anything you authorized with your signature or your partner's signature

Dental plans or medical plans

ACKNOWLEDGEMENTS

It's not often in life you get to work with a great friend on a great project. So here's a huge hug to my co-author and pal, Victoria, who has a unique way of seeing things.

I've had the good fortune to work with the best publishing team in Canada. Thank you to all my HarperCollins peeps, from the people who put the books into stores to the people who correct my dangling participles.

I've been blessed to have editor extraordinaire Kate Cassaday in my life. The woman knows her job cold and has a winsome way of getting exactly what she wants. Kate, with her never-ending questions, has made everything I've written for her better. Since she had the nerve to have a baby midway through this book, I also got to work with Brad Wilson, whose slow and steady hand brought us to the finish line with ease.

As always, a huge hug to my agent, Curtis Russell. Dude, you never disappoint. And I love that you think I'm funny. —G en Gail called to propose this project, I think I screamed, "YES" over the phone.

"Do you want to think about it?" she asked.

"NO!"

Later I called to say, "Gail, my goal is that at the end of this project we like each other even more than we do now."

She replied, "I have no doubt about it."

So thank you for the gift of liking you even more.

I echo Gail's comments about the team that worked so hard to bring about this book. Thank you, and much love for your care. —V